Seamus Heaney

Andrew Murphy

Northcote House

in association with
The British Council

© Copyright 1996 by Andrew Murphy

First published in 1996 by Northcote House Publishers Ltd, Plymbridge House, Estover Road, Plymouth PL6 7PZ, United Kingdom.
Tel: +44 (0) 1752 202300. Fax: +44 (0) 1752 202330.

British Library Cataloguing-in-Publication Data
A catalogue record for this book is available from the British Library

ISBN 0 7463 0783 7

Typeset by PDQ Typesetting, Newcastle-Under-Lyme
Printed and bound in the United Kingdom

Seamus Heaney

SEAMUS HEANEY

for
Andrew Michael

Contents

Acknowledgements viii

Biographical Outline ix

Abbreviations xii

Introduction 1

1 'Living roots awaken in my head': Place and Displacement 8

2 'Where the fault is opening': Politics and Mythology 28

3 'I hear again the sure confusing drum': Reversions and Revisions 48

4 'It was marvellous and actual': Familiarity and Fantasy 69

Postscript 87

Appendix 92

Notes 94

Select Bibliography 98

Index 103

Acknowledgements

I wish to thank Eibhlín Evans, Geraldine Higgins, and John Lucas for the extremely helpful and perceptive comments which they provided on the first draft of my manuscript. Thanks also to Laurie Osborne for supplying materials. I am deeply indebted to Gerard Murphy, whose support and encouragement have sustained my work for many years, and to Charonne Ruth for making it possible and for putting up with it all. Finally, my publishers and I are grateful to Seamus Heaney and Faber and Faber Ltd for permission to quote from the works of Seamus Heaney.

Biographical Outline

1939   Born 13 April, the eldest of nine children. Family
            home is the farm 'Mossbawn', in County Derry,
            Northern Ireland.
1945–51   Attends the local Anahorish School.
1947   UK Education Act makes extended education more
            accessible to the children of less-well-off families. In
            Northern Ireland, specifically, opens up educational
            opportunities for Catholics.
1951–7   Attends, as a boarder, St Columb's College, Derry.
            Among the other graduates of St Columb's are the
            nationalist politician John Hume, left-wing journalist
            Eamonn McCann, literary critic and poet Seamus
            Deane, and the playwright Brian Friel.
1953   Family moves from 'Mossbawn' to a nearby farm
            called 'The Wood', which Heaney's father had
            inherited from an uncle. At about this time, Heaney's
            4-year-old brother, Christopher, is killed in a road
            accident – an incident which the poet writes about in
            'Mid-Term Break'.
1957–61   Attends Queen's University, Belfast. Graduates with
            1st class degree in English Language and Literature.
            Is urged to undertake postgraduate work at Oxford,
            but decides to become a school teacher instead.
1961–2   Attends St Joseph's College of Education,
            Andersonstown, Belfast, and obtains his Teacher's
            Training Diploma. During his time at St Joseph's,
            Heaney writes an extended essay on Northern Irish
            literary magazines and encounters the work of local
            poets such as John Hewitt.

1962	Joins staff of St Thomas's Intermediate School, Ballymurphy, Belfast. The headmaster is the short-story writer Michael McLaverty, who introduces Heaney to the work of the Irish poet Patrick Kavanagh.
1962–3	Part-time postgraduate work at Queen's.
1963–6	Teaches at St Joseph's College of Education.
1963	Philip Hobsbaum establishes Belfast Group. Members include: Michael Longley, Stewart Parker, and James Simmons.
1965	August: marries Marie Devlin. Devlin was born in Ardboe in County Tyrone. She attended St Mary's College of Education in Belfast from 1958 to 1962 and taught at St Columcille's school in County Down.
1966	*Death of a Naturalist* published. Hobsbaum moves to Glasgow; Heaney joins Queen's faculty. Belfast Group continues to meet at Heaney's and includes younger members such as Paul Muldoon, Frank Ormsby, and Michael Foley. July: Heaneys' son Michael born.
1967	Heaney receives the Somerset Maugham Award.
1968	February: second son, Christopher, born. Receives the Cholmondeley Award.
1968–9	Repression of Civil Rights movement prompts a renewal of conflict in Northern Ireland.
1969	*Door into the Dark* published. August: British troops deployed in Derry and Belfast.
1970–1	Teaches as guest lecturer at University of California, Berkeley.
1971	August: internment introduced in Northern Ireland. By the end of the year, a total of 1,576 people have been imprisoned without benefit of trial.
1972	30 January, 'Bloody Sunday': soldiers from the British Army paratroop regiment open fire on unarmed Civil Rights demonstrators in Derry. Thirteen protesters are killed, a further twelve are wounded. August: the Heaneys move to Glanmore, in the Republic of Ireland. Makes his first attempts at translating the medieval Irish poem *Buile Suibhne*. November: *Wintering Out* published.
1973	April: daughter, Catherine Ann, born.

1975   *North* published. Receives the W. H. Smith Award and
        Duff Cooper Prize. October: joins faculty of Carysfort
        Teacher Training College.

1976   November: Heaney and family move to Sandymount,
        near Dublin.

1979   *Field Work* published. Spends a term at Harvard
        University as one of a series of temporary successors
        to the American poet Robert Lowell.

1980   *Preoccupations*, his first collection of essays, published.
        Selected Poems 1965–1975 published.

1980–1 Nationalist prisoners in Northern Ireland stage a
        series of hunger strikes, seeking the reintroduction of
        political (as opposed to criminal) status. Ten prisoners
        would eventually die on the protest, including
        Francis Hughes of Bellaghy, near Heaney's birthplace.

1981   Leaves Carysfort.

1982   January: starts a five-year contract at Harvard, to teach
        one semester a year. Publishes (as co-editor with Ted
        Hughes) an anthology of poems entitled *The Rattle Bag*.

1983   *An Open Letter* published as a pamphlet by Field
        Day in Ireland. The verse letter objects to his work
        being included in an anthology of British poetry. His
        translation of *Buile Suibhne*, entitled *Sweeney Astray*,
        is published in Ireland.

1984   *Station Island* published. *Sweeney Astray* published in
        the UK. Elected to Boylston Chair of Rhetoric and
        Oratory at Harvard. October: mother dies.

1986   October: father dies.

1987   *Haw Lantern* published. Receives the Whitbread
        Award.

1988   *Government of the Tongue*, his second collection of
        essays, published. Becomes Professor of Poetry at
        Oxford University.

1990   *The Cure at Troy*, Heaney's version of Sophocles'
        Philoctetes, performed in Derry and published in
        London. *New Selected Poems* published.

1991   *Seeing Things* published.

1995   October: Heaney awarded the Nobel Prize for
        Literature.

Abbreviations

DD   *Door into the Dark* (London: Faber & Faber, 1969)
DN   *Death of a Naturalist* (London: Faber & Faber, 1966)
FW   *Field Work* (London: Faber & Faber, 1979)
GT   *The Government of the Tongue: The 1986 T. S. Eliot Memorial Lectures and Other Critical Writings* (London: Faber & Faber, 1988)
HL   *The Haw Lantern* (London: Faber & Faber, 1987)
N.   *North* (London: Faber & Faber, 1975)
P.   *Preoccupations: Selected Prose 1968-1978* (London: Faber & Faber, 1980)
SA   *Sweeney Astray* (London: Faber & Faber, 1984)
SI   *Station Island* (London: Faber & Faber, 1984)
ST   *Seeing Things* (London: Faber & Faber, 1991)
WO   *Wintering Out* (London: Faber & Faber, 1972)

I come from scraggy farm and moss,
Old patchworks that the pitch and toss
Of history have left dishevelled.

('A Peacock's Feather', *The Haw Lantern*)

Introduction

Humming
Solders all broken hearts. Death's edge
Blunts on the narcotic strumming.

(Seamus Heaney, 'The Folk Singers' (*DN* 42))

Seamus Heaney begins his second collection of prose writings, *The Government of the Tongue*, with a prefatory essay entitled 'The Interesting Case of Nero, Chekhov's Cognac and a Knocker'. He opens the essay with a telling anecdote. In 1972, he says, he had arranged to meet the singer David Hammond in Belfast in order to go to the BBC studios in the city and put together a tape of songs and poems for a mutual friend of theirs, living in Michigan. In the event, the tape did not get made. As Hammond and Heaney made their way to the studios, the city was rocked by a series of explosions. The air filled with the sound of the sirens of emergency vehicles converging on the city centre. Heaney tells us

> It was music against which the music of the guitar that David unpacked made little impression. So little, indeed, that the very notion of beginning to sing at that moment when others were beginning to suffer seemed like an offence against their suffering. He could not raise his voice at that cast-down moment. He packed the guitar again and we both drove off into the destroyed evening. (*GT*, p. xi)

It is no surprise that Heaney should choose to preface his book with an account of this incident. Reflected in the story, we find some of the central concerns which have both motivated and troubled the poet's career as a writer. Some of these conflicts Heaney himself makes explicit as he proceeds through the essay. Central among them are what Heaney notes as the conflicting demands of Art and Life, or, put another way, of Song and Suffering. On the day in question, Heaney tells us, he and Hammond had felt that their art of song and poetry was

1

simply silenced in the face of the suffering occasioned by the brutal scenes taking shape outside the studio walls. 'What David Hammond and I were experiencing, at a most immediate and obvious level,' he tells us, 'was a feeling that song constituted a betrayal of suffering' (*GT*, p. xii).

In the course of his prefatory essay, and in the pieces that follow it in *The Government of the Tongue*, Heaney comes to revise this view, at least in the sense of rendering it more complex, and seeking to map out a place for poetry in the face of suffering. He both endorses and feels endorsed by the philosophy of the Polish poet, Zbigniew Herbert (who had himself suffered the oppressions of Soviet-dominated Poland), whose poem 'The Knocker' Heaney summarizes as a deceptively simple statement: ' "Go in peace," his poem says. "Enjoy poetry as long as you don't use it to escape reality" ' (*GT*, pp. xviii–xix). Through Herbert, Heaney seeks to strike a delicate balance: between the poet's responsibility to the artifice of his or her own creation and the poet's responsibility to his or her immediate political, historical, and social world.

We might say that Heaney's career has been characterized by a continual negotiation between the various responsibilities of the poet delineated here. Patrick Kavanagh, a fellow Irish poet (whose work greatly influenced Heaney's), once observed of poetry that 'a man . . . innocently dabbles in words and rhymes and finds that it is his life. Versing activity leads him away from the paths of conventional unhappiness.'[1] In Heaney's case, however, we might say that we encounter an instance of a poet who embarks on a literary career dabbling in a certain kind of words and rhymes, dedicated to a certain range of subject matter, but who, as his career progresses, increasingly finds certain political and historical considerations impinging upon him, demanding that he engage with them within the arena of his work. While, at a personal level, poetry may well have led him 'away from the paths of conventional unhappiness', in time historical and political circumstances inevitably led him back to confront a very profound kind of unhappiness: the unhappiness of injustice and loss, of individual and communal grief. In more specific terms, we might say that Heaney begins his career by fashioning himself as a poet very much in the mould of Kavanagh: a poet concerned with what Heaney himself has called, in discussing Kavanagh, 'the unregarded data of the usual life' (*GT* 7). Like Kavanagh, Heaney set out as a poet seeking both to celebrate and to scrutinize the contours of such a life. As a Catholic growing up and living in the Protestant-dominated Northern Ireland statelet, however, political considerations very frequently pulled at the fabric of the 'usual life' that Heaney experienced, ultimately straining it to breaking point.[2]

A poem such as 'A Constable Calls' from Heaney's fourth volume, *North*, allusively registers the subtle ways in which Heaney's community was subjected, as part of its experience of day-to-day life, to a system of power from which its members felt alienated. At first reading, the poem seems to trace a relatively genial, bureaucratic visit to the Heaneys' farm by a local police constable. On closer inspection, however, we find that throughout the poem there runs a note of fear of the policeman's authority, and the poem's vocabulary persistently carries an ominous note of the brutal force held available to be exercised by this agent of the state (the dynamo on the policeman's bicycle is 'cocked back', like the hammer of a gun; the bicycle's pedals are momentarily 'relieved | Of the boot of the law'; most explicitly, the child narrator stares at 'the polished holster | With its buttoned flap, the braid cord | Looped into the revolver butt' (*N* 60)). In the final image of the poem, we are told that, leaving the farm, the policeman's 'boot pushed off | And the bicycle ticked, ticked, ticked' (*N* 61). As the poem closes, then, the ticking hub of the bicycle wheel conjures up an image of the timing device of a bomb, ticking its way down to the moment of explosion.

In a way, we can say that that ominous repetitive ticking of an explosion waiting to happen runs quietly but persistently through Heaney's early career as a poet. Though, in his first two published volumes, Heaney mostly preoccupies himself with a Kavanagh-inspired engagement with 'the unregarded data of the usual life', both volumes contain a small number of poems which advert in some way to the situation in Northern Ireland. As the 1960s drew to a close, a radical change occurred in the 'usual life' that formed the clearest focal point of Heaney's poetic vision in that decade. The anticipated explosion came at the turn of the decade when the Northern state finally collapsed into continuous crisis, and the conflict in the province intensified and became progressively more and more bloody. At mid-career, Heaney found himself expected – and expecting himself – to address that crisis in his poetry. In *Wintering Out* (1972), *North* (1975), and *Field Work* (1979), Heaney returns again and again to the contemporary political situation, seeking ways to address it, to confront it in his work.

In a sense, then, having started his career in the manner of a Patrick Kavanagh, Heaney, at mid-career, found himself cast in something like the role of another Irish predecessor poet: W. B. Yeats. In 'Among School Children', Yeats describes himself as 'A sixty-year-old smiling public man',[3] and, as the situation in his homeland progressively deteriorated, Heaney too found himself thrust into the role of a public figure. His discomfort at his new high-profile status is registered in 'Exposure', placed at the very end of *North*:

> How did I end up like this?
> I often think of my friends'
> Beautiful prismatic counselling
> And the anvil brains of some who hate me
>
> As I sit weighing and weighing
> My responsible *tristia*.

> (*N*. 66)

Just as Yeats struggled to come to terms with another moment of crisis in Ireland in poems like 'September 1913', 'Easter 1916', 'The Rose Tree', and 'Meditations in Time of Civil War', so Heaney struggled to find an adequate way of addressing the conflicts of his particular historical moment in the poems he wrote and published from the early 1970s to the mid-1980s. Again like Yeats, he not only struggled to find expression for and poetic engagement with the political crisis, but also worried over the question of the nature of the poet's responsibility to that political situation.[4] What, both men wondered, was the role of the poet in and towards such times of crisis? In both men we find an anxiety concerning the relationship between the contemplative, essentially passive life of the poet and the active life of those who become directly involved in the affairs of the world. The point is made most forcefully by Yeats, perhaps, in his poem 'In Memory of Major Robert Gregory'. Killed in air combat in the

4

First World War, Gregory is the epitome for Yeats of the informed, self-conscious man of action:

> Some burn damp faggots, others may consume
> The entire combustible world in one small room
> As though dried straw, and if we turn about
> The bare chimney is gone black out
> Because the work had finished in that flare.
> Soldier, scholar, horseman, he,
> As 'twere all life's epitome.
> What made us dream that he could comb grey hair?[5]

By contrast with the brightly burning flame of the engaged, active life, the smokey 'damp faggots' nourished by the isolated poet may seem absurdly irrelevant, casting a pitifully wan light upon the world.

By the time Heaney came to publish *The Government of the Tongue* in 1988, however, he had made his peace with many of these issues. His rendering of Herbert's 'A Knocker' is indicative of how this accommodation has been reached: ' "Go in peace," his poem says. "Enjoy poetry as long as you don't use it to escape reality." ' The poet, in other words, must walk a fine line between commitment to the formal, aesthetic pleasures of the text and commitment to the social and political world in which the poem is composed, neglecting neither, acknowledging the force of both.

The desire to hold such contradictory impulses together is entirely characteristic of the latest phase of Heaney's career and is registered in the titles of two of his most recent publications. Take *The Government of the Tongue*, for instance. On the one hand, as Heaney himself notes, the title indicates the 'aspect of poetry as its own vindicating force. In this dispensation, the tongue (representing both a poet's personal gift of utterance and the common resources of language itself) has been granted the right to govern' (*GT* 92). On the other hand, he notes, 'my title can also imply a *denial* of the tongue's autonomy and permission. In this reading, "the government of the tongue" is full of monastic and ascetic strictness' (*GT* 96). Following on from the logic of this latter proposition, Heaney finds himself asking 'What right has poetry to its quarantine? Should it not put the governors on its joy and moralize its song?' (*GT* 99). The phrase 'the government of the tongue' thus holds together in fragile unity these two opposing positions (the right of poetry to an aesthetic autonomy; the necessity of subordinating poetry to political or moral constraints) and it is to just such a fragile unity that Heaney pledges fidelity.

We find the same doubleness in the title of Heaney's 1991 collection of poems, *Seeing Things*, which posits a visionary power in poetry, enabling us to '[squint] out from a skylight of the world' (*ST* 57), to achieve 'a pitch | | Beyond our usual hold upon ourselves' (*ST* 86). And yet, even as poetry allows us to achieve this transcendent vision, to 'see things' as we have not seen them before, the title also acts as a kind of brake on the possibility of our granting blind allegiance to such transcendent envisioning. As the title warns us, such transcendent sight may be no more than simply 'seeing things' – a self-deception in thinking we perceive what in fact does not exist at all. It is on this thin line between faith and scepticism that Heaney balances his later poetry.

Heaney himself ends the article with which we began this introduction by quoting from one of his own poems – 'The Singer's House', written for David Hammond. In the concluding stanza of the poem, Heaney writes:

> When I came here first you were always singing,
> a hint of the clip of the pick
> in your winnowing climb and attack.
> Raise it again, man. We still believe what we hear.
>
> (*GT*, p. xxiii; *FW* 27)

The poem was written in the wake of the abortive Belfast recording session which had been planned with Hammond. In a sense, it registers Heaney's ultimate belief in the necessity and value of the poetic act – his belief that, perhaps they ought, after all, to have continued with the session, despite the horrific events taking place outside the studio walls. But it is a hard-won belief. As he writes elsewhere in *The Government of the Tongue*:

Here is the great paradox of poetry and of the imaginative arts in general. Faced with the brutality of the historical onslaught, they are practically useless. . . . In one sense the efficacy of poetry is nil – no lyric has ever stopped a tank. In another sense, it is unlimited. It is like the writing in the sand in the face of which accusers and accused are left speechless and renewed. (*GT* 107)

This complex view neatly indicates the trajectory of Heaney's career as a poet. His early faith in poetry is unconflicted. He revels in what he calls the 'primitive delight in finding world become word' (*GT* 8). In mid-career, he is brought into confrontation with 'the brutality of the historical onslaught' and struggles with the question of how he might encounter it in his work. The effect of this encounter is ultimately to renew his faith in poetry, but that faith is now tempered by a knowledge of poetry's desperate limitations; by a recognition that the transcendence that poetry offers is never more than tentative – an inscription in the sand that the incoming tide will surely obliterate. But, for all that, the force of poetry is still valid, still, in some fragile way, efficacious. As Heaney says in 'The Singer's House': 'We *still* believe what we hear.' Possibly we do not believe with quite the same innocent conviction as might once have been possible, but we do still believe.

1

'Living roots awaken in my head': Place and Displacement

Seamus Heaney first began publishing his poems during his time as an undergraduate at Queen's University in Belfast, when a number of pieces by him appeared in various student magazines. In 1963 he became a member of Philip Hobsbaum's 'Belfast Group', an informal gathering of young writers who would meet regularly at Hobsbaum's Belfast home to critique each other's work. Hobsbaum greatly admired Heaney's poetry and he exercized his influence to secure Heaney an entry into the London publishing world. Through these contacts, Heaney was eventually offered a contract with Faber & Faber, who published his first volume of poems, *Death of a Naturalist*, in 1966, and who have remained his primary publishers ever since.

The poem which opens *Death of a Naturalist* is 'Digging'. It not only appears on the opening page of this volume, but also takes its place as the first poem in Heaney's *Selected Poems* (1980) and his *New Selected Poems* (1990). Heaney indicates his sense of the poem's significance when he writes in *Preoccupations* that:

> 'Digging', in fact, was the name of the first poem I wrote where I thought my feelings had got into words, or to put it more accurately, where I thought my *feel* had got into words. ... I wrote it in the summer of 1964, almost two years after I had begun to 'dabble in verses'. This was the first place where I felt I had done more than make an arrangement of words: I felt that I had let down a shaft into real life. (*P.* 41)

As Heaney indicates here, he views 'Digging' as marking some-
thing like a point of departure for his career as a poet. We might
say that this is true not only in terms of the poem's formal
achievement in translating, as Heaney puts it, 'feeling into
words', but also in the sense that 'Digging' registers, in small
compass, many of the themes and concerns that would domi-
nate his early poetry, in addition to providing an early glimpse
of certain other issues that would surface as important elements
later in his writing.

The language of 'Digging' introduces us to what will become,
for much of his career, Heaney's dominant register. We can hear
this verbal style at play in the next to last stanza of the poem,
where Heaney writes:

> The cold smell of potato mould, the squelch and slap
> Of soggy peat, the curt cuts of an edge
> Through living roots awaken in my head.

(DN 2)

Heaney deploys several verbal effects here to forge an evocative
image of his subject. We find alliteration in 'the squelch and
slap | Of soggy peat' and 'curt cuts'; assonance, a run of similar
vowel sounds, in 'The cold smell of potato mould'; and ono-
matopoeia in 'squelch' and 'slap', which echo the sounds they
describe. This kind of precise wielding of language to evoke a
strong sense of the sight and sound of the world being described
is entirely characteristic of Heaney's poetry and indicates the
early influence on Heaney of the Victorian poet Gerard Manley
Hopkins and also of Heaney's near contemporary, the English
poet, Ted Hughes. A similar set of effects is at play throughout
Death of a Naturalist. Take, for instance, the following lines from
the title poem of the collection:

> Bubbles gargled delicately, bluebottles
> Wove a strong gauze of sound around the smell.

(DN 3)

and

> their loose necks pulsed like sails. Some hopped:
> The slap and plop were obscene threats. Some sat
> Poised like mud grenades, their blunt heads farting.

(DN 4)

As Neil Corcoran has observed of this poem, 'the sheer noise Heaney manages to make out of English vowels here is remarkable – a dissonant cacophony that forces the mouth to work overtime if the reader speaks the lines aloud'.[1] Language is thus deployed here with enormous precision in order to evoke a detailed image of a very specific world.

Where, verbally, we can trace the influence of Hopkins and Hughes in this early work, thematically we can register the influence that fellow Irish poet Patrick Kavanagh has had on Heaney's career. In an article on Kavanagh's poetry entitled 'The Placeless Heaven', included in *The Government of the Tongue*, Heaney writes of his excitement at first encountering Kavanagh's work:

> When I found 'Spraying the Potatoes' in the old *Oxford Book of Irish Verse*, I was excited to find details of a life which I knew intimately – but which I had always considered to be below or beyond books – being presented in a book. The barrels of blue potato spray which had stood in my own childhood like holidays of pure colour in an otherwise grey field-life – there they were, standing their ground in print. (*GT* 7)

Just as Kavanagh took as his subject matter his local native world of rural Monaghan, so Heaney in his turn renders in his poetry images of the life and landscape of the farming community where he grew up. Thus 'Digging' memorializes the cycles of manual labour on his family's farm – digging up potatoes and cutting turf on the bog. The titles of other poems in his first two collections point to a similar engagement with local issues and concerns. In *Death of a Naturalist* we find 'The Barn', 'Blackberry-Picking', 'Dawn Shoot', 'At a Potato Digging', 'Cow in Calf', and 'In Small Townlands', and in *Door into the Dark* we find 'The Forge', 'Thatcher', 'Rite of Spring', and 'Whinlands'. In a poem such as 'Churning Day' from *Death of a Naturalist* we can see Heaney's meticulous attention to detail as he attempts to recreate an exact image of the traditional local practices of butter-making:

> Out came the four crocks, spilled their heavy lip
> of cream, their white insides, into the sterile churn,
> The staff, like a great whisky muddler fashioned
> in deal wood, was plunged in, the lid fitted.
> My mother took first turn, set up rhythms

that slugged and thumped for hours. Arms ached.
Hands blistered. Cheeks and clothes were spattered

with flabby milk.
                    Where finally gold flecks
began to dance. They poured hot water then,
sterilized a birchwood-bowl
and little corrugated butter-spades.

                                        (*DN* 9)

We notice the painstaking accumulation of details here – the specificity of 'The staff ... fashioned | in deal wood', the 'birchwood-bowl' and the 'corrugated butter-spades' – and, again, there is the evocative precision of much of the language used (the 'rhythms | that slugged and thumped for hours', for instance). Andrew Waterman has aptly observed of 'Churning Day' that 'reading the poem leaves one feeling that one has made the butter oneself'.[2]

These poems are, however, more than simply evocative descriptions. In common with Kavanagh, in memorializing the world of the familial and the local, Heaney is also attempting to work through the nature of his relationship to that world. In a revealing comment in 'The Placeless Heaven', Heaney observes that 'Kavanagh's genius had achieved singlehandedly what I and my grammar-schooled, arts-degreed generation were badly in need of – a poetry which linked the small farm life which produced us with the slim-volume world we were now supposed to be fit for. He brought us back to where we came from' (*GT* 9). Heaney thus sees Kavanagh as offering a link between the world of poetry and the local world of 'small farm life'. His comment indicates a certain alienation from this latter world which has resulted from his generation's having become 'grammar-schooled' and 'arts-degreed'. What Heaney is pointing to here is the fact that his generation was the first to benefit from the UK's 1947 Education Act, which significantly broadened access to secondary and university education, making it easier for students from less prosperous backgrounds to remain within the educational system for much longer than would traditionally have been the case. While access to education broadened the horizons of such students, it also served in some measure to alienate them from their communities and families, which, like

11

the Heaneys, in very .many cases did not have a tradition of participating in advanced-level education.

'Digging' is itself centrally concerned with this issue of alienation and the need somehow to negotiate the distance between origins and present circumstances. Recalling his writing of 'Digging', Heaney remembers, in *Preoccupations*, the comments of the adults on neighbouring farms as he made his way to and from school: 'invariably they ended up with an exhortation to keep studying because "learning's easy carried" and "the pen's lighter than the spade" ' (*P.* 42). In the poem, 'learning' and the privileges to which it provides access are what separates the speaker from his father. The speaker sits inside, looking out at his father working beneath his window. In this sense, we might say that the growing cultural distance between the two is marked by the physical distance of their relative positions inside and outside the house, high at the window, low on the ground. Similarly, the shift in the speaker's class position (from the difficult circumstances of small farm life to educated middle-class security) is registered in the privileged position occupied by the speaker, as he has the luxury of being able to sit by and observe his father labouring outside.

The speaker in the poem experiences his privilege as effecting a kind of disjunction, emblematized by his relationship to the act of digging. In the narrative of the poem, digging serves to establish a sense of historical continuity: the father's digging now, in the poem's present, shifts easily to his 'com[ing] up twenty years away | Stooping in rhythm through potato drills | Where he was digging' (*DN* 1). This past activity of the father is in turn linked to the work of prior generations, following the same course in life: 'By God, the old man could handle a spade. | Just like his old man.' In his youth, the speaker in the poem has had a relationship of sorts to this extended tradition. He recalls, twenty years ago, picking up the potatoes unearthed by his father's digging:

> He rooted out tall tops, buried the bright edge deep
> To scatter new potatoes that we picked,
> Loving their cool hardness in our hands.

The appreciation for the feel of the newly exposed potatoes indicates a sense of connectedness between the boy and his environment. In a similar vein, the speaker in the poem recalls having 'carried . . . milk in a bottle | Corked sloppily with paper' to his grandfather as he worked cutting turf 'on Toner's bog'. In both these instances, while the child figure's role is in some senses peripheral to the main activity of digging, he is, none the less, connected with that activity and with the traditional continuities that it signals. By contrast, the adult speaker feels entirely *disconnected* from this world. As an adult, he should be expected to take his place in the labouring line of his father and grandfather ('Just like his old man', as it were), but, instead, he is forced to observe: 'I've no spade to follow men like them' (*DN* 2).

Appropriately enough, we might think, the poet's recourse in these circumstances is to metaphor, as he concludes his poem by offering an analogy between the pen and the spade:

> Between my finger and my thumb
> The squat pen rests.
> I'll dig with it.

What Heaney suggests here is that the work he undertakes as a poet can be a kind of 'labour' of the same order as the work which has, for generations, been undertaken by his forebears. In this sense, though the poet cannot take his place in the extended line of labouring generations, he can, nevertheless, preserve the continuities represented by that line by encompassing that world within his poetry. If he cannot literally dig, he can 'dig' metaphorically, unearthing the details of the life of his family and community and honouring them by preserving them in his verse.[3]

In *Preoccupations*, Heaney offers us a more explicit rendering of the analogy between poetry and rural labour when he notes that ' "Verse" comes from the Latin *versus* which could mean the turn that a ploughman made at the head of the field as he finished one furrow and faced back into another' (*P.* 65). Heaney turns this scholarly perception to practical effect in 'Follower' – another poem from *Death of a Naturalist* in which the poet contemplates his relationship with his father. Heaney describes his father in 'Follower' as

> An expert. He would set the wing
> And fit the bright steel-pointed sock.

13

> The sod rolled over without breaking.
> At the headrig, with a single pluck
>
> Of reins, the sweating team turned round
> And back into the land.

(DN 12)

Heaney effects an immediate consonance here between his own unfolding act of poetic composition and his father's work with the plough. Where, in *Preoccupations*, Heaney registers an equivalence between the end of the ploughed furrow and the end of the poetic line, here the two physically mirror each other in the neat enjambment (that is, the 'turn over' from one poetic line into the next) of 'the sweating team turned round | And back into the land', where the turn of the verse itself matches exactly the turning of the horses it describes. Elsewhere in the poem, Heaney contrives similar effects, as in the case of the endstopped 'The sod rolled over without breaking.' – a line composed of a single sentence which, just like the unbroken turned sod it describes, maintains its own integrity (rather than, for instance, running on into the next line, as in the case of 'the sweating team turned round | And back ...'). Again, the 'single pluck | | Of reins' occurs across a stanza break, reflecting the momentary drag and stay which pulls the horses round.

Viewed in this light, 'Follower' might appear to be a perfect formal enactment of the pledge which Heaney offers at the end of 'Digging': 'Between my finger and my thumb | The squat pen rests. | I'll dig with it.' Synthesizing metaphor and practice, he turns his pen here into a ploughshare; he effects a consonance between his poetic labour and the labour of his family and community and, in the process, he memorializes that labour in verse. As the poem draws to a close, however, we discover an unexpected note of disjunction emerging, as Heaney writes:

> I wanted to grow up and plough,
> To close one eye, stiffen my arm.
> All I ever did was follow
> In his broad shadow round the farm.
>
> I was a nuisance, tripping, falling,
> Yapping always. But today
> It is my father who keeps stumbling
> Behind me, and will not go away.

Despite the confident closure and paradigm of continuity established in 'Digging' and formally enacted throughout the early stanzas of 'Follower', then, the same conflicts which we found initially troubling the poet in 'Digging' endure here. In particular, we note the re-emergence of a generational conflict as the speaker is unable to establish an adequate relationship with his father. He finds their roles reversed, as he feels the weight of his father metaphorically dragging along behind him, just as he himself had literally dragged along behind his father when he was a child. The speaker is thus positioned in the poem between a sense of himself as a child, dependent on his father, and a mature sense of himself, struggling to establish his independence from his father and from his family generally.

A great many poems in *Death of a Naturalist* concern themselves with such moments of transition from childhood to maturity and, more particularly, with the cost incurred in acquiring the knowledge that puts an end to childhood innocence.[4] 'Death of a Naturalist', 'The Barn', 'An Advancement of Learning', 'Blackberry Picking', and 'Dawn Shoot' are just some of the poems that take up this theme. In 'The Barn' something menacing lurks within the dark confines of a farm building – a threat which the fearful speaker in the poem is unwilling and unable to encounter: 'I lay face-down to shun the fear above. | The two-lugged sacks moved in like great blind rats' (*DN* 5). In 'An Advancement of Learning', the poem which immediately follows 'The Barn' in *Death of a Naturalist*, the speaker *does* confront his fear, symbolized once again as a rat, this time encountered on a riverbank:

> The tapered tail that followed him,
> The raindrop eye, the old snout:
> One by one I took all in.
> He trained on me. I stared him out
>
> Forgetting how I used to panic
> When his grey brothers scraped and fed
> Behind the hen-coup in our yard,
> On ceiling boards above my bed.
>
> (*DN* 7)

In confronting his fear on this occasion, the speaker achieves a victory – the rat is forced into retreat and the speaker, still holding his ground, 'stare[s] a minute after him'. The fruits of his victory are emblematically marked in the closing line of the poem, in which Heaney observes: 'Then I walked on and crossed the bridge'. This crossing of the bridge is clearly indicative of the successful negotiation of a certain 'rite of passage'. Having confronted his fear and triumphed, the speaker is free to move on to another stage in his journey.

'An Advancement of Learning' has a certain jubilant, jocular tone to it, as the speaker easily wins his battle of wills and emerges triumphant from his mock-heroic struggle with his emblematic adversary. 'Death of a Naturalist', by contrast, presents a much more conflicted and troubled picture. The first half of the poem produces an idyllic sense of an early springtime childhood, enjoyed within a beneficent natural order. The closing lines of this first section, however, signal an impending change, as they register a shift from the upbeat, positive 'yellow in the sun' to the dark and ominous 'brown | In rain' (*DN* 3) – an effect all the more marked by the fact that 'In rain' is set as a single line. In the second section of the poem, the frogspawn that has been gathered in section one comes to maturity and the natural world the speaker had enjoyed is overrun by adult frogs, which repulse him: 'I sickened, turned, and ran' (*DN* 4). As the narrative of the maturing of the frogspawn indicates, one of the fears registered in the poem is a fear of maturity itself – especially of sexual maturity. A strong thread of sexual imagery runs through the second section of the poem, as the frogs thicken the air with a 'bass chorus', sit 'cocked on sods', making 'obscene threats', 'their blunt heads farting'. As Michael Parker has observed, by the end of the poem 'innocent delight at the "warm thick slobber" has been replaced by disgust at his body's "spawn" '.[5] The narrative of the poem resists both maturity itself and an emerging sexual sense of self.

If 'Death of a Naturalist' is a poem about the difficult transition from childhood to adolescence, and the simultaneous fascination and repulsion of sexual awakenings, many of the later poems in Heaney's first collection concern themselves with a more fully adult transition – from the independence of single life to the responsibilities of marriage. Heaney's turning to such subject matter is not too surprising, given that just a year before *Death of a Naturalist* was published he had married Marie

Devlin, a fellow Northern Irish schoolteacher. As in the earlier poems in the collection, many of the marriage pieces concern themselves with the crossing of a threshold from one state of life to another. The uncertainties of the threshold state itself – where one lingers between one positioning and the next – are nicely caught in a poem such as 'Honeymoon Flight'. Here the airborne transition between two points of a journey reflects the moment of suspension between an old life left behind and a new life in prospect:

> And launched right off the earth by force of fire,
> We hang, miraculous, above the water,
> Dependent on the invisible air
> To keep us airborne and to bring us further.
>
> (DN 36)

The stanza holds together the four traditional elements of earth, fire, water, and air, in an act of balance mirroring that achieved by the aircraft itself in flight. As the poem draws to a close, the horizon of a new life opens up. The poem ends: 'Air-pockets jolt our fears and down we go. | Travellers, at this point, can only trust.' At a literal level, of course, the 'trust' in question here is being placed in the pilot of the aircraft, to bring it in safely to land, but it also indicates the trust that must be placed in the married state itself, to fulfill the lives of the individual partners.

The most striking of the marriage poems included in *Death of a Naturalist* is a short piece entitled 'Lovers on Aran'. Heaney has often been (justly) criticized for deploying male/female binaries in his poems in a manner which presents the female as passive, yielding, accepting – the powerless recipient of an active, dominating, dynamic male. As Patricia Coughlan has observed, frequently in his poems Heaney 'constructs an unequivocally dominant masculine figure, who explores, describes, brings to pleasure and compassionates a passive feminine one'.[6] In 'Lovers on Aran', however, in a set of interesting inversions and reversals, Heaney actually presents an interrogation of these very gender stereotypes. He begins with an image of the waves swarming in 'To possess Aran' (DN 34). But the act of possession signalled is an odd one, as the waves come in to take their possession 'from the Americas'. The 'geography' of this image is logical enough – the Atlantic waves wash in eastward onto

17

the shores of the Aran islands, which lie off the west coast of Ireland. But, in addition to the geography, there is also a historical reference at play here. The thrust of colonial possession has always been westward, not eastward. Historically (especially in the sixteenth and early seventeenth centuries), Ireland frequently served as a staging point for colonizing expeditions setting out to possess the Americas. Here, in an inversion of historical precedent, the direction of possession is reversed – the waves flow from the New World to possess a corner of the Old. We might also notice that, whereas Heaney most typically associates water – fluid, yielding, formless – with the passive female (see, for instance, 'Undine' and 'Rite of Spring' in *Door into the Dark*), here the water is initially given a certain masculine value, being presented as, essentially, 'penetrating' the land. But these alignments are quickly complicated. Having detailed the sea's act of possession, Heaney asks:

> Or did Aran rush
> To throw wide arms of rock around a tide
> That yielded with an ebb, with a soft crash?

This cancels the active, aggressive image of irruption, as the inflow of the waters may constitute as much an act of enfolding by the land as of penetration by the sea. Having thus rendered the alignments and significances of his imagery ambiguous, Heaney goes on to ask: 'Did sea define the land or land the sea?' – an unanswerable question which presents the lovers as united in a relationship of mutuality and equality. In the broader sweep of the poem, the question leaves fruitfully open issues of definition and identity, in a way that will not be typical of much of Heaney's other poetry in which the issue of gender is prominently featured.

'Lovers on Aran' is one of two poems set on the islands in *Death of a Naturalist*, the other being one of the last poems in the collection, entitled 'Synge on Aran'. This latter poem is concerned with the Irish playwright, John Millington Synge, who, between 1898 and 1902, spent long periods on the islands. Synge's project as a dramatist was to provide an accurate picture of rural life in Ireland and to find a way of reproducing in English some of the rhythms, textures, and nuances of the Irish language. Heaney conceives of him with

> a hard pen
> scraping in his head;
> the nib filed on a salt wind
> and dipped in the keening sea.
>
> (*DN* 39)

Just as Heaney imagines himself in 'Digging' as adapting his own pen to the unearthing task of the spade, so here he imagines Synge as fashioning *his* pen upon the environment he wishes to describe – sharpening his nib on the abrasive wind, the mournful sea his ink.

This image of Synge at the end of *Death of a Naturalist* takes us back to Heaney's other important literary precursor, Patrick Kavanagh. As it happens, Kavanagh had little time for Synge. He felt that Synge and his privileged middle-class Protestant literary colleagues lacked, as outside observers, any true connection with the realities of country life and simply romanticized the figure of the peasant and grossly misrepresented life as it was actually lived in rural Ireland (a point most forcibly made in Kavanagh's poetry in *The Great Hunger*). For all that, there is much that unites Kavanagh, Synge, and Heaney as writers from three different generations seeking to accomplish certain things within their work. Both Synge and Kavanagh pledge a certain fidelity to the precise details of the purely local, believing that, if one is faithful to such local concerns, they will of themselves open outwards to something greater, something more universal in its significance. Kavanagh draws a distinction between 'provincialism', on the one hand, and 'parochialism', on the other. 'A provincial', he writes, 'is always trying to live by other people's loves, but a parochial is self-sufficient.' Kavanagh's clearest statement of faith in the parochial in his poetry is delivered in his well-known poem, 'Epic'. In this poem, Kavanagh remembers a particular dispute in his native area which inflamed local passions intensely. Recollecting that the events took place on the eve of the Second World War, he yields to a moment of self-doubt, wondering whether these local incidents can be said to be in any way significant in the face of such great upheaval. As the poem draws to a close, however, this doubt is banished and his faith in the local is reaffimed:

> That was the year of the Munich bother. Which
> Was more important? I inclined

> To lose my faith in Ballyrush and Gortin
> Till Homer's ghost came whispering to my mind.
> He said: I made the Iliad from such
> A local row. Gods make their own importance.[7]

The great epic of the *Iliad*, the story of the Trojan War, is here reduced to its origins as 'a local row' – a petty dispute, we might say, between the Greek Menelaus and the Trojan Paris over which of them should have Menelaus' wife, Helen. It is the very act of poetic memorialization itself, Kavanagh suggests (through Homer), that lends the local story its significance, that creates the epic, drawing the universal from the particular.

We have already noted the significance of Kavanagh's poetic practice to Heaney earlier in this chapter when we discussed Heaney's attempt to encompass his domestic world within his poetry and thereby to effect a sense of continuity with his community and to work through the nature of his relationship to his origins. Kavanagh's broader perspective on the nature and function of poetry is also of great relevance to Heaney's work, especially as he begins both to develop further and to move beyond the themes which we have seen him explore in *Death of a Naturalist*. In an early comment on Kavanagh, in an article published in the *Listener*, Heaney observed that 'Kavanagh enhances our view of the world, and makes us feel that any task, in any place, is an important act, in an important place',[8] and, in Heaney's second and third collections, *Door into the Dark* and *Wintering Out*, we find several poems in which, like Kavanagh, he focuses upon the minute particularities of the local in order to expose within them traces of a greater world. 'The Forge' from *Door into the Dark* is a case in point. It opens with the line 'All I know is a door into the dark' (*DD* 7) which, in addition to giving the collection its title, also resonates with the very last line of *Death of a Naturalist*, where, in 'Personal Helicon', Heaney proclaims that he writes poetry in order 'to set the darkness echoing' (*DN* 44). The connection between the two poems is significant, as Heaney often ends one collection of his work with a piece which, in effect, will serve as a sort of 'manifesto' for the collection to follow.

The opening line of 'The Forge' seems to indicate that what Heaney's poetic art gives him is a point of penetration into the heart of a world which is beyond the everyday, but which proves to be somehow simultaneously central to it. By contrast with 'The Barn', where the speaker in the poem is unwilling to enter into the darkness, afraid of what he might find there, the speaker in 'The Forge' seeks to go into the darkness, to see what lies beyond, or *within*, the outside world. What he finds is indeed something that 'sets the darkness echoing' – the hammer-blows of the blacksmith working a new horseshoe upon his anvil, set at the centre of the forge. Heaney brings his usual eye for detail to bear on the blacksmith in the poem, as, in a few short but evocatively accurate strokes, he provides us with a pen picture of him: 'leather-aproned, hairs in his nose, I He leans out on the jamb . . . Then grunts and goes in.' The ordinariness of this picture comes as something of a surprise and contrasts with the exotic creatures Heaney's earlier poetic speaker imagined inhabited the darkness of 'The Barn' – 'bright eyes' staring 'From piles of grain in corners, fierce, unblinking', 'bats . . . on the wing', 'two-lugged sacks . . . like great blind rats'. The smith's peripheral and oddly anachronistic status is registered in the poem when Heaney sketches an image of him, in his momentary rest from his work, recalling 'a clatter I Of hoofs where traffic is flashing in rows'. The horse having been superseded by the car, the smith is, in this context, a representative of a dying trade. But even as he is presented as ordinary, peripheral, outdated in the poem, the smith is also centralized, just as his anvil is centred within the forge itself. He is consciously imagined within the poem as a figure for the poet-as-maker, a figure not unlike that of another 'blacksmith' – the Hephaestus of the Homeric epics who, though crippled and cuckolded, is capable of producing work of great beauty and intricacy and who, crucially, is able to encompass an entire universe on the decorative surface of a single shield, when asked by Thetis to forge armour for her son Achilles:

> Five welded layers
> composed the body of the shield. The maker
> used all his art adorning this expanse.
> He pictured on it earth, heaven, and sea,
> unwearied sun, moon waxing, all the stars
> that heaven bears for garland . . . [9]

Heaney's smith, as he is like Homer's Hephaestus, is also, we might say, like Kavanagh's Homer, in that he is the one who forges enduring significance from base material, beating 'real iron out', expending 'himself in shape and music', and creating a whole world within small compass.

The poem which follows 'The Forge' in *Door into the Dark* – 'Thatcher' – charts a very similar sort of trajectory. Again the poem concerns a practitioner of a dying trade – the job of the thatcher is to tend to the traditional roofwork of cottages that are covered in straw, or 'thatch', an increasing rarity as more and more rural homes are modernized. The tools, materials, and techniques of this skilled craftsman are meticulously described in the poem. The thatcher turns up

> Unexpectedly, his bicycle slung
> With a light ladder and a bag of knives.
> He eyed the old rigging, poked at the eaves,
>
> Opened and handled sheaves of lashed wheat-straw.
> Next, the bundled rods: hazel and willow
> Were flicked for weight, twisted in case they'd snap.
>
> (*DD* 8)

Like the blacksmith, the thatcher is a figure for the creative intelligence who, though peripheral and rather outmoded, is nevertheless capable of producing from the ordinary ('straw . . . rods . . . a white-pronged staple . . . sods') something extraordinary, something wondrous:

> Couchant for days on sods above the rafters,
> He shaved and flushed the butts, stitched all together
> Into a sloped honeycomb, a stubble patch,
> And left them gaping at his Midas touch.

Robert Welch has noted the connection between Heaney's 'Thatcher' and the sixteenth-century English poet Sir Philip Sidney's theoretical treatise *A Defence of Poetry*, in which Sidney, contrasting the works of art and of nature, comments that, where nature's 'world is brazen [i.e. made of brass], the poets only deliver a golden' world.[10] Both Sidney, then, and Heaney (through the figure of the thatcher with his 'Midas' touch) posit a transformative, alchemical power for poetry: the power to take the ready material of the everyday and to fashion it into something astounding. In a sense we might say that 'The Forge' and 'Thatcher' represent Heaney's own 'Defence of Poetry', his own version of Kavanagh's 'Epic', in which he affirms the power of poetry to transform, to find in the everyday and the particular something greater, something more significant.

If 'The Forge' and 'Thatcher' are, then, in some sense 'theoretical' poems, signalling a kind of poetic manifesto, in other poems in *Door into the Dark* and *Wintering Out* we find that theory put into practice. This is particularly true of the group of 'place-name' poems which Heaney includes in the second of these collections – 'Anahorish', 'Toome', and 'Broagh' (whose very titles are taken from place-names) and also 'Gifts of Rain' and 'A New Song'. In these poems, Heaney unites a theory of poetry with a theory of language itself. On the one hand, following Kavanagh, Heaney believes that poetry can find something greater than the particular in the local; on the other, from another Irish poetic source – the ancient native Irish poetic tradition of *dinnseanchas* – he derives a sense that the language of local naming bears within itself a kind of compressed narrative of local history. Just as Kavanagh believes that an engagement with the particularities of the local can open outwards to a greater world, so the *dinnseanchas* tradition suggests that a kind of etymological investigation of local naming can open up the greater history of the named place.

In *Preoccupations* Heaney writes of 'the cultural depth-charges latent in certain words and rhythms':

> that binding secret between words in poetry that delights not just the ear but the whole backward and abysm of mind and body ... the energies beating in and between words that the poet brings into half-deliberate play ... the relationship between the word as pure vocable, as articulate noise, and the word as etymological occurrence, as symptom of human history, memory and attachments. (*P*. 150)

This captures the essence of Heaney's view of the *dinnseanchas* tradition: his belief that language itself – and, specifically, the language of proper naming – carries within itself a kind of native history, an etymologically etched memory. We can see this notion at play in 'Anahorish', the first of the place-name poems from *Wintering Out*. The name 'Anahorish' is an anglicized conflation of the native Irish *anach fhíor uisce* and Heaney begins his poem with a translation of the Irish, as he writes: 'My "place of clear water" ' (*WO* 6).[11] From this unveiling of the literal meaning of 'Anahorish', Heaney, in a move that might remind us of

Kavanagh, goes on to posit the place of his origins as a kind of primally original place, as it becomes

> the first hill in the world
> where springs washed into
> the shiny grass
>
> and darkened cobbles
> in the bed of the lane.

From here, Heaney returns to the name itself, atomizing it, considering its constituent parts: 'Anahorish, soft gradient | of consonant, vowel-meadow'. Heaney believes that he finds here, in the phonetic elements of the word itself, an image of the very landscape to which the name is attached, as consonant and vowel combine to reflect the rise and fall of the land.

In the final two stanzas, the poem opens up, moving from the specificities of geography to the residues of history. Faintly perceived human figures enter the landscape which the first two stanzas have established. At first they seem virtually an effect of the name itself, as Heaney writes

> *Anahorish*, soft gradient
> of consonant, vowel-meadow,
>
> after-image of lamps
> swung through the yards
> on winter evenings.

The place-name itself triggers a residual image not of the inhabitants of the place but of the lights which they carry. In the closing lines of the poem the inhabitants themselves finally emerge into the light, but even now they are seen obscurely, through a mist:

> With pails and barrows
>
> those mound-dwellers
> go waist-deep in mist
> to break the light ice
> at wells and dunghills.

What Heaney has offered us in the poem, then, is a process whereby, through scrutinizing the particularities of a proper name, we are able to understand its meaning, its connection to its place of application, and its position of centrality. Beyond the geography of this linguistically demarcated place, we are able to catch a glimpse of its human history. Through the rough glass of the name we can see an image of the original, ancient inhabitants of the place.

Heaney angles for analogous effects in the other place-name poems included in *Wintering Out*. In 'Gifts of Rain', the name of the local river, Moyola, is imagined as offering a similar self-image as that perceived in 'Anahorish': 'The tawny gutteral water I spells itself: Moyola I is its own score and consort' (*WO* 15). The name offers a kind of internal harmony, redolent of local affairs: 'reed music, an old chanter I I breathing its mists through vowels and history.' Some of the specificities of the 'history' evoked here begin to emerge in 'Toome', 'A New Song', and 'Broagh'. In 'Toome' we find Heaney exploring a name which has a lightly explosive quality as it is spoken: 'My mouth holds round I the soft blast-ings, I *Toome, Toome*' (*WO* 16). As Heaney digs down through its history, pushing 'into a souterrain I prospecting', he unearths the remnants of history. In among the bric-à-brac of forgotten daily lives – the 'loam, flints', 'fragmented ware', and 'fish-bones' – he finds 'musket-balls', a token of the country's explosive and conflictual past.

The contours of that past and Heaney's sense of how the narrative of history is intertwined with language itself emerge in 'A New Song'. In this poem, the speaker encounters a native of Derrygarve and the place-name spurs the poet to his usual local analysis. As in the case of 'Anahorish', 'Derrygarve' calls up through Heaney's *dinnseanchas* machinery potent images of local geography. The poem turns, however, around the fulcrum of its middle stanza, where Heaney writes:

> And Derrygarve, I thought, was just,
> Vanished music, twilit water,
> A smooth libation of the past
> Poured by this chance vestal daughter.
>
> (*WO* 23)

Where in 'Anahorish' the trajectory of the poem is to open out towards a vision of an ancient community which, while faintly perceived, is nevertheless imagined as living in the flow of daily life ('break[ing] the light ice I at wells and dunghills'), here, in 'A New Song', we register an image of a life that is imagined as irretreviably past. In contrast with 'Gifts of Rain', where the Moyola is 'A swollen river' echoing an active and regenerative

25

'mating call of sound', the same river here presents a 'twilit water' and the general feeling of the stanza is of an irreversible dwindling and fading – from twilight towards the darkness of endless night, as it were. Reading the poem allegorically, we can see it as registering, up to this point, a lament for a native culture that has been lost as a result of Ireland's colonial history. Native Irish civilization is, in this regard, little more than a 'vanished music'. As the poem moves into its final two stanzas, however, a significant shift occurs:

> But now our river tongues must rise
> From licking deep in native haunts
> To flood, with vowelling embrace,
> Demesnes staked out in consonants.
>
> And Castledawson we'll enlist
> And Upperlands, each planted bawn –
> Like bleaching-greens resumed by grass –
> A vocable, as rath and bullaun.

What Heaney presents here is, in fact, a narrative of *decolonization*. The native language returns to supplant the language that banished it – overrunning the imperial 'demesnes' and 'consonants' (Heaney has written in *Preoccupations* that he thinks 'of the personal and Irish pieties as vowels, and the literary awarenesses nourished on English as consonants', (*P*. 37)) and displacing the alien imposed names of 'Castledawson' and 'Upperlands'. Heaney's image for this displacement is the repossession of the 'bleaching-greens' (emblematic of the linen industry introduced into the north of Ireland by Protestant colonists) by the native grass (symbolic of the native Irish pastoral farming tradition) – a taking back of the land from the colonist. The final word in the poem is literally given to the native, as Heaney invokes the Irish 'rath' and 'bullaun'.

If 'A New Song' is in some measure charged with the energy of nationalist, anti-colonialist aspiration, Heaney offers us a rather different aspiration in 'Broagh'. Neil Corcoran has observed of 'Broagh' that it 'has a significance in Heaney's work altogether disproportionate to its length',[12] and it is certainly true that this short poem is immensely rich and resonant. In the second and third stanzas of the poem Heaney offers his usual reading of geography into the place-name ('the shower | gathering in your heelmark | was the black O | | in *Broagh*' (*WO* 17)). In the first stanza, however, we get something rather different from the standard *dinnseanchas* performance:

> Riverba[n]k,[13] the long rigs
> ending in broad docken
> and a canopied pad
> down to the ford.

Heaney is being immensely precise in his choice of language here. The opening word of the poem offers a translation of 'broagh' itself, which is an anglicized version of the Irish *bruach*, meaning 'riverbank'. Heaney ends this first line, however, with the word 'rigs' – meaning 'furrows' – a word brought to the north of Ireland by seventeenth-century Scots colonists. Elsewhere in this same stanza Heaney offers us the dialect words 'docken' and 'pad', both of which, again, have strong connections with Scots. What Heaney creates in this first stanza then, is a kind of common language community that unites colonizer and native.

This union is thrown into relief in the closing stanza of the poem, where Heaney comments on the pronunciation of *broagh*, noting 'that last | *gh* the strangers found | difficult to manage'. The harsh-sounding final phoneme of 'Broagh' indicates a sound that has been largely lost within the English language, but which is still available to native and colonizer alike in the language community of the north of Ireland. Linguistically, then, the correct pronunciation of 'Broagh' serves simultaneously to unite the divided communities of the North and to set them apart from the alien community of the English, divided from them by sea and sound, as it were. What Heaney seems to be offering is an image of the union of the two traditions of the North – an internal union which detaches the territory from its union with England.

These poems in *Wintering Out* offer two perspectives on the fraught political and historical situation in the north of Ireland. When *Wintering Out* appeared in 1972, that situation had reached a point of crisis. As a northern poet, Heaney felt a responsibility to respond to that crisis in some way in his writing. 'A New Song' and 'Broagh' are indicative of Heaney's efforts to address the central political and historical issues of the day. In the next chapter we will examine his response to the political crisis in greater detail.

2

'Where the fault is opening': Politics and Mythology

Wintering Out opens with a poem of dedication to David Hammond and the Northern Irish poet Michael Longley:

> This morning from a dewy motorway
> I saw the new camp for the internees:
> a bomb had left a crater of fresh clay
> in the roadside, and over in the trees
>
> machine-gun posts defined a real stockade.
> There was that white mist you get on a low ground
> and it was déjà-vu, some film made
> of Stalag 17, a bad dream with no sound.
>
> Is there life before death? That's chalked up
> on a wall downtown. Competence with pain,
> coherent miseries, a bite and sup,
> we hug our little destiny again.
>
> (*WO*, p. v)

As a point of entry into Heaney's third collection of poems, this piece (later incorporated into 'Whatever You Say Say Nothing' in *North*) offers us a glimpse of a very different world from the one we are introduced to on the opening page of *Death of a Naturalist*. Where 'Digging' presents us with a natural, rural world of 'flowerbeds', 'potato drills', 'new potatoes', 'good turf', and 'living roots' (*DN* 1, 2), Heaney's poem for Hammond and Longley brings us face to face with a harsh new set of realities. Northern Ireland had changed quite dramatically between 1966, when *Death of a Naturalist* was published, and 1972, when

Wintering Out appeared, and many of these changes are registered here in this poem of dedication.

As the 1960s ended, the Northern Irish state lurched towards crisis. With the failure of the Civil Rights movement, militant nationalism (and militant unionism) revived and the province grew accustomed both to the sounds and to the consequences of bombings and shootings. As Heaney drives along the motorway (in itself something of an incongrous intrusion of the modern world into his typical poetic *mise-en-scène* – at least up to this point in his career), he sees the crater which a bomb has scarred into the landscape. As a result of the deepening crisis, the British Army were now deployed in the North and they, too, intrude into the scene, with their 'machine-gun posts defin[ing] a real stockade'. In August of the previous year the government had introduced internment without trial, and hundreds of people (almost all of them Catholics) had been rounded up and detained in camps like the one that Heaney sees from the motorway. The whole scene has, for the poet, an air of unreality about it. Hardly able to believe that the situation can have come to this, he likens what confronts him to a scene from a bad war movie.

For all the shock of encountering this scene, however, the final stanza of the poem registers less surprise at new developments than resignation in the face of the recognizably familiar. The slogan chalked up on a Belfast wall – 'Is there life before death?' – indicates a certain grim humour, the kind of weary cynicism that comes from bitter familiarity with suffering. In the closing lines of the poem, an entire community settles down to the desperate mundanity of the reopened wounds of old conflict.

Though Heaney finds himself brought into direct confrontation with the latest manifestation of this conflict as he opens *Wintering Out*, in fact, if we look back through both *Door into the Dark* and *Death of a Naturalist*, we can trace the pulse of that conflict even in his earliest work. It is no coincidence, we might feel, that, even in 'Digging', Heaney's pen is imagined first as a gun before it becomes a spade ('Between my finger and my thumb | The squat pen rests; snug as a gun' (*DN* 1)). Such images are surprisingly insistent throughout his early poems. In 'Churning Day', for instance, 'the four crocks' stand in the small pantry like 'large pottery bombs' (*DN* 9); in 'Trout', the fish 'Hangs, a fat gun-barrel', 'his muzzle gets bull's eye', his food is 'torpedoed', he 'darts like a tracer- I bullet', 'A volley of cold blood I I ramrodding the current' (*DN* 26); 'In Small Townlands' presents us with the following lines: 'The spectrum bursts, a bright grenade, I When he unlocks the safety catch I On morning dew, on cloud, on rain' (*DN* 41). What we discover here is an assimilation of the language of conflict into the metaphoric register of the poems.

Elsewhere in the early poems Heaney addresses the issue of the conflict itself more directly. 'At a Potato Digging' and 'For the Commander of the *Eliza*' in *Death of a Naturalist*, and 'Requiem for the Croppies' from *Door into the Dark*, are all poems which take up aspects of the history of the conflict in Ireland. The first two poems concern themselves with the Great Famine (1845–51), when perhaps a million people died as a result of the failure of the potato crop in Ireland in several successive years. In 'At a Potato Digging' Heaney opens with a description of a contemporary farming scene: 'A mechanical digger wrecks the drill', churning up the potatoes, as a group of 'Labourers swarm in behind' (*DN* 18) to gather in the crop. In the third section of the poem, however, the scene shifts and we are presented with a stark image of the famine victims of the previous century:

> Live skulls, blind-eyed, balanced on
> wild higgledy skeletons,
> scoured the land in 'forty-five,
> wolfed the blighted root and died.
>
> . . . . .
>
> Mouths tightened in, eyes died hard,
> faces chilled to a plucked bird.
> In a million wicker huts,
> beaks of famine snipped at guts.

> (*DN* 19)

As the section draws to a close, we are returned to the contemporary scene, but with the knowledge that, beneath the surface of this modern world, lies the unhealed wound of the famine experience: 'where potato diggers are, I you still smell the running sore' (*DN* 20).

In the immediately following poem in *Death of a Naturalist*, 'For the Commander of the *Eliza*', Heaney takes up the question of where political responsibility for the tragedy of the famine

30

lies. Following the work of the historian Cecil Woodham-Smith, he implicitly rejects the view that the famine deaths are merely to be ascribed to natural causes, finding, instead, a certain culpability in the calculated inaction of the colonial authorities. The poem is dedicated to the captain of a coastguard boat who encounters six starving Irishmen adrift in a small rowboat. They beg him for food and he refuses, but later, haunted by the image of the 'Six wrecks of bone and pallid, tautened skin' (*DN* 21), he reports the incident to his Inspector General, who orders a better distribution of relief to famine victims in the area, and receives a reprimand from the government authorities in London for his trouble. The poem closes with the Captain's ironic rendering of London's response:

> Let natives prosper by their own exertions;
> Who could not swim might go ahead and sink.
> 'The Coast Guard with their zeal and activity
> Are too lavish' were the words, I think.
>
> (*DN* 22)

The lack of compassion and concern exhibited by the authorities in 'For the Commander of the *Eliza*' serves to symbolize the consequences of Ireland's colonial experience and the suffering which it occasioned. In 'Requiem for the Croppies' Heaney takes up the other side of the colonial equation – the history of Irish resistance to colonial domination. The poem was written in 1966, when the fiftieth anniversary of the 1916 uprising (which eventually led to partial independence for Ireland) was being celebrated. 'Requiem' does not deal directly with the uprising, but rather harks back to another revolutionary moment – the 1798 rebellion, which was suppressed with great ferocity by the British. Heaney focuses on an incident from the uprising when a large group of 'croppies' (young fighters who cut their hair short in imitation of the peasants in the French Revolution) made a last-ditch stand against the British on Vinegar Hill in County Wexford and were cut down, defeated by the superior technology of British weaponry: 'Terraced thousands died, shaking scythes at cannon' (*DD* 12). In closing the poem, however, Heaney offers an image of regeneration: 'They buried us without shroud or coffin | And in August the barley grew up out of the grave.' In *Preoccupations*, Heaney offers his own gloss on these lines:

The poem was born of and ended with an image of resurrection based on the fact that some time after the rebels were buried in common graves, these graves began to sprout with young barley, growing up from barley corn which the 'croppies' had carried in their pockets to eat while on the march. The oblique implication was that the seeds of violent resistance sowed in the Year of Liberty [1798] had flowered in what Yeats called 'the right rose tree' of 1916. (P. 56)

What Heaney seeks to do, then, in 'Requiem for the Croppies' is to effect a sense of historical continuity between Irish acts of resistance across the centuries – from the uprising of 1798 to that of 1916. In another poem from *Death of a Naturalist*, 'Docker', he engages less with the historical sweep of the conflict as it has played itself out throughout the island than with the bigotry and barely contained sectarian violence of the Northern Ireland he has experienced in his own lifetime. The poem presents a portrait of a working-class Protestant engaged in Belfast's notoriously discriminatory shipbuilding industry. He fancies this figure as utterly unyielding, built of steel, just like the vessels he spends his life working on. His hatred of Catholics is registered in the second stanza of the poem:

> That fist would drop a hammer on a Catholic –
> Oh yes, that kind of thing could start again.
> The only Roman collar he tolerates
> Smiles all round his sleek pint of porter.
>
> (*DN* 28)

'Docker' is uncharacteristically explicit in its engagement with the situation in the North. Heaney himself has associated the poem with 'the slightly aggravated young Catholic male part' of his temperament which he says he suppressed elsewhere in his early poetry in favour of 'the private county Derry childhood part' of himself.[1] The poem is, however, strikingly prophetic, with its expectation that sectarian conflict could well be revived in the North.

Writing of the eventual outbreak of that anticipated revival of conflict in 1969 and of his response to it as a poet, Heaney observes in *Preoccupations* that

> From that moment the problems of poetry moved from being simply a matter of achieving the satisfactory verbal icon to being a search for images and symbols adequate to our predicament. . . . I felt it

imperative to discover a field of force in which, without abandoning fidelity to the processes and experience of poetry ... it would be possible to encompass the perspectives of a humane reason and at the same time to grant the religious intensity of the violence its deplorable authenticity and complexity. (*P.* 56–7)

In pursuing this 'search for images and symbols adequate to our predicament', Heaney found himself drawn to a book entitled *The Bog People*, written by P. V. Glob and published in an English translation in Northern Ireland's watershed year of 1969. As Heaney himself notes, the book 'was chiefly concerned with preserved bodies of men and women found in the bogs of Jutland, naked, strangled or with their throats cut, disposed under the peat since early Iron Age times' (*P.* 57). Heaney was attracted to the book because it both served to focus a number of his traditional interests, and also offered him a particular frame of reference and set of symbols which he could deploy in engaging with the present conflict and its antecedent history.

The attractions of an account of the preservative and historically retentive powers of bogland to the author of a poem such as 'Digging' should be obvious. In *Preoccupations*, indeed, Heaney imagines 'Digging' itself as having been 'dug up', rather than written, observing that he has 'come to realize that it was laid down in me years ago' (*P.* 42). In this sense, the poetic act is one of 'retrieval' – of recovering something that already exists – rather than of creating something entirely new from whole cloth. This notion of retrieving what has been preserved but occluded resonates with Heaney's sense of the tradition of *dinnseanchas*. In the place-name poems, we remember, Heaney sought to excavate the hidden histories which are compacted in a local name. Bogland, in fact, provides a perfect analogy for this sense of the relationship between locale and history, since bogland literally preserves material elements of a particular region's past, yielding them up when the land is excavated. As Heaney observes in *Preoccupations*, bog serves as 'the memory of the landscape, or as a landscape that remember[s] everything that happened in and to it' (*P.* 54). Heaney gives his clearest poetic expression to this idea in a poem entitled 'Kinship' from *North*, in which he characterizes bogland as

Ruminant ground,
digestion of mollusc

and seed-pod,
deep pollen-bin.

Earth-pantry, bone vault,
sun-bank, embalmer
of votive goods
and sabred fugitives.

Insatiable bride.
Sword-swallower,
casket, midden,
floe of history.

(N 34)

Bogland is presented here as an insatiable and consuming ground that indiscriminately swallows all that comes to it and preserves it intact, as a kind of treasure trove to be yielded up in time.

Heaney's first attempt at exploiting the poetic potential of the symbolism of bogland comes in a poem of that very name, which closes *Door into the Dark*. The positioning of the poem at the end of the collection is significant, since, as in the case of *Death of a Naturalist*'s 'Personal Helicon', it serves to indicate a significant direction Heaney will pursue in his future work. The preservative power of the bog is graphically indicated in the third stanza of 'Bogland', where the massive frame of an Irish deer rises up out of the land:

They've taken the skeleton
Of the Great Irish Elk
Out of the peat, set it up
An astonishing crate full of air.

(DD 41)

In contrast to the grandeur of this image, the next object to emerge from the bog in the poem is butter, an everyday domestic necessity, 'recovered salty and white'. Taken together, the elk and the butter signify the heterogeneity of the bog, its tendency to preserve everything, without selecting out a particular set of objects. In the closing stanzas of the poem we learn that the process of excavation is potentially endless. The layers of the bog lead to no final resting place, but simply reveal a bottomless centre:

Our pioneers keep striking
Inwards and downwards,

> Every layer they strip
> Seems camped on before.
> The bogholes might be Atlantic seepage.
> The wet centre is bottomless.

(DD 41–2)

Heaney returns to the theme of preservation and the deep world to which it gives access in *Wintering Out*. He first takes up the issue in 'Bog Oak', a poem not about the bog itself, but about a piece of seasoned wood, retrieved from the bog and used as building material. The speaker in the poem remembers the beam as 'a cobwebbed, black | long-seasoned rib | | under the first thatch' (*WO* 4), indicating that it has served as a roof-beam in his own family home. In the manner of some of the place-name poems, the memory of this rafter calls up images of an entire native community – not just the speaker's own immediate family but, we sense, a gathering of his ancestors stretching back into a communal past. The poem offers us a kind of cinematic effect, as we move from the interior of the family dwelling to the door, where we are presented with a view through the 'mizzling rain' to 'the far end | of the cart track'. In the final two stanzas of the poem, we discover what is just about visible at the end of that track:

> Perhaps I just make out
> Edmund Spenser,
> dreaming sunlight,
> encroached upon by
>
> geniuses who creep
> 'out of every corner
> of the woodes and glennes'
> towards watercress and carrion.

(WO 4–5)

Heaney offers us here a dense and complex vision. What the speaker sees is an image of the sixteenth-century English poet Edmund Spenser, who served as a minor colonial official in Ireland. Because of his service to the government, Spenser was able to acquire, cheaply, a large amount of property, including an estate at Kilcolman, in County Cork. While living at Kilcolman, Spenser wrote his famous poem *The Faerie Queene* and also composed a political treatise on Irish affairs, entitled

35

A View of the Present State of Ireland, in which he advocated the deployment of extremely harsh measures against the native Irish.

As Michael Parker makes clear,[2] the connection back to Spenser is related to the central image of the poem. The colonizing schemes of the early modern era led to the extensive clearing of woodland areas, and we can presume that it is a piece of this cleared wood which emerges from the bog in the opening of the poem as 'A carter's trophy' to be 'Split for rafters'. 'Bog Oak', then, offers us a similar set of connections as 'At a Potato Digging'. Where the earlier poem suggests that, if we penetrate the surface of the contemporary rural landscape, we will find the unhealed wound of the Great Famine, 'Bog Oak' indicates that we can read the colonial history of the country within the grains of the retrieved timber. The sense of historical resonance is compounded by the quotation from Spenser's *View* which Heaney incorporates into his poem. In the treatise itself, the full passage appears as follows:

> Out of every corner of the woodes and glinnes they came creeping foorthe upon theyr handes, for theyr legges could not beare them; they looked like anatomyes of death, they spake like ghostes crying out of theyr graves; they did eate of the dead carrions, happy were they yf they could finde them, yea, and one another soone after, insoemuch as the very carcasses they spared not to scrape out of theyr graves; and yf they founde a plotte of water-cresses or shamrokes, there they flocked as to a feast . . .[3]

Spenser is writing of the famine in Munster which resulted from English campaigns against the Irish in the late sixteenth century, but we can hardly fail to hear an echo here, again, of the famine of the mid-nineteenth century, in which identical events played themselves out. Karl Marx has famously observed that 'all great world-historical facts and personages occur, as it were, twice. . . . the first time as tragedy, the second as farce',[4] but here we find history repeating itself not as tragedy and farce but as endlessly reiterated cycles of affliction and blight.

It is this sense of the repetition of cycles rooted deep in the past that attracted Heaney to Glob's book on *The Bog People*. What Glob offers is an image of a pre-Christian, northern European tribal society, in which ritual violence is a necessary part of the structure of life. Most of the Iron Age bodies recovered from the Jutland bogs and documented by Glob had been the victims of ritual killings, many of them having served as human sacrifices to the earth goddess Nerthus. Heaney detected a kinship between the pagan civilizations of Jutland and Ireland's own Celtic traditions and saw, as Michael Parker puts it, 'the fatal attraction of Nerthus liv[ing] on in such figures from the Nationalist pantheon as Kathleen ni Houlihan [Caitlín ní Houlihán], the Shan Van Vocht [Shean Bhean Bhocht], and Mother Ireland'.[5] In an interview with Brian Donnelley in 1977, Heaney articulated his sense of the force of the Iron Age narratives as a means of establishing a space in which it was possible for him to encounter contemporary atrocities which, otherwise, he did not feel he could adequately encompass within his poetry:

> My emotions, my feelings, whatever those instinctive energies are that have to be engaged for a poem, those energies quickened more when contemplating a victim, strangely, from 2000 years ago than they did from contemplating a man at the end of the road being swept into a plastic bag – I mean the barman at the end of our road tried to carry out a bomb and it blew up. Now there is of course something terrible about that, but somehow language, words didn't live in the way I think they have to live in a poem when they were hovering over that kind of horror and pity.[6]

Heaney makes his sense of the connections between Ireland and Jutland explicit in *Wintering Out* in a four-line poem entitled 'Nerthus'. The first brief stanza of the poem provides a symbolic image of the goddess – a rib of ash wood 'staked in peat' (*WO* 38). The rib is forked and is marked with an incision to represent the female genitalia: 'Its long grains gathering to the gouged split'. Neil Corcoran has observed of the second stanza of the poem – 'A seasoned, unsleeved taker of the weather, | Where kesh and loaning finger out to heather' – that it 'implicitly translates the goddess out of Iron Age Jutland into modern Northern Ireland [as] the landscape she stands in is defined in the terms of Northern dialect – "kesh", a causeway, and "loaning", an uncultivated space between fields'.[7] As Corcoran notes, the invocation of 'kesh' has a particular modern resonance, since it was at 'Long Kesh' (now the Maize Prison) that many of the North's political prisoners were held.

Heaney's first extended attempt at conflating his sense of Glob's Jutland rituals with his own sense of mythic and modern Irish history comes in 'The Tollund Man' – the poem which

precedes 'Nerthus' in *Wintering Out*. The 'Tollund Man' is one of
the recovered bodies featured by Glob in his book. He was a
victim sacrificed to Nerthus, in the hope of securing a good crop
from the land, and it is in this sense that he is, as Heaney describes
him, 'Bridegroom to the goddess' (*WO* 36). Heaney imagines the
killing of the Tollund Man and his subsequent burial in the bog
as a kind of violent love-making between victim and goddess, in
which Nerthus, 'open[ing] her fen', preserves the victim's body
by immersing it in her sexual 'dark juices'. When the Tollund Man
is dug up, many centuries later, the turf-cutters discover 'His last
gruel of winter seeds | Caked in his stomach'. As a sacrificial
victim to the goddess of germination, then, he carries the poten-
tial of germination (his 'gruel of winter seeds') within himself,
rather in the manner of the young fighters in 'Requiem for the
Croppies' whose 'graves began to sprout with young barley,
growing up from barley corn which [they] had carried in their
pockets to eat while on the march' (*P*. 56).

In the second section of the poem, Heaney makes the connec-
tion between Jutland and Ireland explicit. If Jutland has had its
victims, so too has Heaney's own native place. And in Ireland,
too, the killings have a certain ritualistic dimension to them;
Heaney recalls an incident in which the bodies of four young
Catholics, murdered by Protestant militants, were dragged along
a railway line in an act of mutilation:

> Tell-tale skin and teeth
> Flecking the sleepers
> Of four young brothers, trailed
> For miles along the lines.

> (*WO* 37)

Heaney imagines that, if he addresses a prayer to the Tollund
Man ('risk[ing] blasphemy' as a Christian by aligning himself
with the rituals of a pagan religion), then perhaps the potential
for germination and regeneration inherent in the Tollund Man's
sacrifice, and in his very body (buried with its freight of seed),
might be released, not in the victim's native ancient Jutland, but
in contemporary Ireland. It might 'make germinate | | The scat-
tered, ambushed | Flesh' of the North's sacrificial victims.

In the final section of the poem, Heaney imagines paying
a visit to the museum in Aarhus where the Tollund Man has

been placed on display. Though the names of the region he passes through ('Tollund, Grabaulle, Nebelgard') will be alien to him, and the local language unintelligible, he fancies that, as an Irishman burdened with the weight of his country's history, he will feel a kinship with a landscape that has witnessed similar conflict and killings. As he writes in the precisely balanced closing stanza of the poem:

> Out there in Jutland
> In the old man-killing parishes
> I will feel lost,
> Unhappy and at home.

Heaney's most intense engagement with the Northern conflict occurs in his 1975 collection, *North*. Formally, much of *North* continues the trend towards shorter lines of verse, initiated in *Wintering Out*, as Heaney exploits further what Bernard O'Donoghue has referred to as 'the "artesian stanza", the short-lined poems that Heaney used to drill down metaphorically into his territory's and his consciousness's prehistory'.[8] Heaney observed at the time that he sought 'to take the English lyric and make it eat stuff that it has never eaten before . . . like all the messy and, it would seem, incomprehensible obsessions in the North'.[9]

North is continuous with *Wintering Out* thematically as well as formally in that we are offered further bog poems in the collection, but Heaney also broadens the northern European connection as he recollects Ireland's Viking history and draws upon the *Njal's Saga* as a source of mythological resonances. In 'Funeral Rites' Heaney begins with an autobiographical meditation on his experience of death as he grew up in the country. The funerals he remembers are not distinguished as being of particular people – the most specific detail he offers is that he lifted the coffins 'of dead relations' (*N*. 6). What dominates the opening section of the poem is a sense of the rituals and ceremonies which have been established in the family and the local community for encountering and assimilating the experience of death, for grieving and for resuming the flow of everyday life. Each funeral follows a routine pattern and the bodies of the dead take on a uniform appearance:

> their eyelids glistening,
> their dough-white hands
> shackled in rosary beads.
>
> Their puffed knuckles
> had unwrinkled, the nails
> were darkened, the wrists
> obediently sloped.

In this last image, we get a sense of death's having virtually been wrought into submission, as the disposition of the corpse conforms to the requirements of formal arrangement.

As the first section of the poem comes to an end, the sense of repetitive formality and religious ritual is reinforced: we are told that '*always*, in a corner, | the coffin lid, its nail-heads dressed | | with little gleaming crosses' (*N.* 7; emphasis added). The section concludes with a certain hint of regret, but with a definite sense of closure and completion:

> Dear soapstone masks,
> kissing their igloo brows
> had to suffice
>
> before the nails were sunk
> and the black glacier
> of each funeral
> pushed away.

There is a certain poignancy in the cold kiss delivered to the unyielding flesh before the coffin lid is hammered in place, but this is the way of '*each* funeral' and once the ritual is complete, death can be 'pushed away' and life resumed.

What the first section of the poem gives us, then, is a sense of death's having been encompassed by ritual in a way that makes the flow of life itself possible. The second section of the poem presents a stark contrast to this settled, cyclical world. In section II, we enter the contemporary realm of the Northern conflict, where the natural rhythms of the community are disrupted by the rise of sectarian violence, leading to what Heaney calls, in a disturbingly evocative phrase, 'neighbourly murder'. While the poet desires a reinstatement of old routines, observing

> we pine for ceremony,
> customary rhythms:

the temperate footsteps
of a cortège, winding past
each blinded home

there is also a recognition here that the deep-running fissures of the conflict could never be healed by means of such easy, familiar pieties. Something more elemental, more deeply rooted in the historical fibres of the community, is required. It is for this reason that Heaney offers his vision of a single great funeral, arising out of the north and heading for 'the great chambers of Boyne' in the Irish midlands. Once again, what Heaney provides us with here is a densely interwoven set of compacted references. Just as the Nerthus cult of Glob's *Bog People* takes us back to pre-Christian Europe, so the burial chambers of the megalithic site of Newgrange, in the Boyne Valley, takes us back to pre-Christian Ireland. In the native Celtic religion, the Boyne was a sacred river, 'the fountain of all knowledge', and the Newgrange site itself was associated with Aengus, the Celtic god of love.[10] The Boyne has other associations too, however, since it was at the Battle of the Boyne in 1690 that the Catholic James II suffered a decisive defeat at the hands of the Protestant William of Orange, who would succeed him on the English throne. As the historian Roy Foster has observed: 'Ireland's peculiar conditions imposed an Irish configuration on the confrontation; in history and ballad . . . the war . . . was the last stand of Catholic Ireland against Protestant Ascendancy, imparting the epic aura still immortalized in the naïve art of Belfast gable-ends.'[11]

Heaney's restoration of the Boyne's Celtic associations thus takes us back past contemporary and historical conflict to a point in mythic history where reconciliation of enduring conflict can be effected. This point is made explicit in the closing section of the poem, where Heaney imagines the end of the funeral, with the mourners returning northwards. As they drive north, they pass by 'Strang and Carling fjords' (*N.* 8) – a reference to Ireland's Viking history, detected in the Irish place-names of 'Strangford' and 'Carlingford'. This memory of Ireland's Norse connections summons up in turn, in the closing stanzas of the poem, an uncharacteristic moment of quiescence and harmony from the epic Icelandic *Njal's Saga*. Heaney imagines the Irish victims his poem has carried to rest in Newgrange as being 'disposed like Gunnar' (*N.* 9) – himself a victim of the *Saga's* remorseless cycles of revenge. The aftermath of Gunnar's death is untypical in the story and has a particular resonance for the situation in Ireland. He lay, we are told, 'beautiful | inside his burial mound, | though dead by violence | | and unavenged'. Gunnar thus lies at rest, even though his allies have effected no vengeance killing against his enemies in reprisal for his death. His story thus provides an instance of the cycle of revenge killings being broken and offers hope for Ireland at a time when the cycle of sectarian murders appears interminable. The poem ends with an image of peaceful resolution, as Gunnar rises within his tomb, serene and untroubled:

> Men said that he was chanting
> verses about honour
> and that four lights burned
>
> in corners of the chamber:
> which opened then, as he turned
> with joyful face
> to look at the moon.

The vision which Heaney offers here of easy reconciliation and sublime peacefulness is, however, not sustained throughout the volume as a whole. Much more characteristic of *North*'s troubled register and remit is a piece such as the much discussed bog poem 'Punishment', where Heaney engages with the contemporary conflict through the lens of his trope of bog retrieval. As in the case of 'The Tollund Man', Heaney's point of departure here is again a photograph from Glob's *The Bog People*. In this case, it is a picture of a young woman who had likely been shorn, stripped, killed, and thrown into the bog as a punishment for adultery. 'Punishment' is, throughout, an uneasy poem, which seems deeply uncertain both of its own motives and of its ability to achieve any point of equilibrium or certainty. This uneasiness is registered in the opening stanzas of the work, when the poet begins by expressing a sense of identification and empathy with the victim, but very quickly becomes a voyeur (as he explicitly admits in a later stanza of the poem), exercising his male power to take pleasure in the woman's exposed and subjected body:

> I can feel the tug
> of the halter at the nape

> of her neck, the wind
> on her naked front.
>
> It blows her nipples
> to amber beads,
> it shakes the frail rigging
> of her ribs.

(N. 30)

The conflict indicated here is both given further expression and compounded later in the piece, in the poet's direct address to the dead woman. 'My poor scapegoat', he writes, 'I almost love you | but would have cast, I know, | the stones of silence' (N. 31). Heaney conflates pagan and Christian mythologies here, as the story of the Jutland victim is combined with the story of the woman caught in adultery included in the Christian Gospel According to St John. The poet indicates that, his attraction to the woman notwithstanding, he would have been complicit in her death, if not directly, then certainly by failing to raise his voice in support of her or in protest at her punishment. In the closing stanzas of the poem, this sense of troubled complicity in an act of violence is extended from its immediate focus in the poet's contemplation of this Iron Age victim to the circumstances of the contemporary conflict in Northern Ireland, as the poet characterizes himself as one who has

> stood dumb
> when your betraying sisters,
> cauled in tar,
> wept by the railings,
>
> who would connive
> in civilized outrage
> yet understand the exact,
> and tribal, intimate revenge.

Like 'Funeral Rites', this poem too takes up the question of revenge. But the revenge in question is effected within the community itself, rather than between two opposing communities. The woman victim retrieved from the bog provides an image for those young Catholic women in Heaney's own Northern Ireland subjected to 'tarring and feathering' by members of their own community. The punishment was most often inflicted on those who became involved with members of the British Army. Like

43

Glob's female victim, the women typically had their heads shaved, before having hot tar and feathers poured over them and being left tied up in a public place, as an act of ritual humiliation.

The poet's response to the contemporary punishment, like his response to its Iron Age analogue, is conflicted and ambiguous. On the one hand, he 'connive[s] | in civilized outrage', deploying the kind of non-commital liberal attitude that he anatomizes later in *North*, in 'Whatever You Say Say Nothing': ' "Oh, it's disgraceful, surely, I agree," | "Where's it going to end?" "It's getting worse" ' (*N.* 52). On the other hand, he again finds himself complicit in the act of retribution, as he admits that he is able to understand (and, by extension, in some measure to sympathize with) the rationale for the punitive act. The punishment is characterized as 'exact | and tribal' – it is presented as being precisely calibrated – 'justified' in a literal sense – and as having its roots deep in the ancestral mindset of the community, being therefore in some sense inevitable and unavoidable.

The ambivalence which Heaney displays here about the 'exactness' of 'tribal' violence is registered elsewhere in the first part of *North* also. In the closing section of 'Kinship', for example, Heaney calls upon the Roman historian, Tacitus, to be a witness to the situation in Ireland. Tacitus mentions Ireland in his *Agricola* and he devotes a chapter to the cult of Nerthus in his *Germania*. Once again blending the contemporary with the mythical, Heaney, addressing Tacitus, offers him material for another study of the Nerthus cult. 'Our mother ground' he writes 'is sour with the blood | of her faithful, | they lie gargling | in her sacred heart'. Where the original devotees of Nerthus offered sacrificial victims to her in the hope of increasing the fertility of the land, here the glut of corpses serves merely to sour the soil. In closing the poem, Heaney exhorts Tacitus to 'Read the inhumed faces'

> of casualty and victim;
> report us fairly,
> how we slaughter
> for the common good
>
> and shave the heads
> of the notorious,
> how the goddess swallows
> our love and terror.

> (*N.* 38–9)

Blake Morrison has observed of these lines that they are one of the
moments in *North* where, 'like it or not', Heaney's 'poetry grants
sectarian killing in Northern Ireland a historical respectabil-
ity which it is not usually granted in day-to-day journalism:
precedent becomes, if not a justification, then at least an "explana-
tion" '.[12] While one might quibble with the details of Morrison's
judgement here (not least with the faith he seems to place in
'day-to-day journalism'), nevertheless, his broader point is well
taken: as in the case of 'Punishment', the violence here appears
to have a certain air of inevitability about it. The source of the
current troubles, Heaney seems to be suggesting, lies deep in
mythic history, where ineluctable cycles have been set in motion.
In a dangerous elision, 'love' and 'terror' seem also to become
inextricably entwined, as the goddess of the earth 'swallows' both
without distinction.

'Punishment' and 'Kinship' both offer gendered images of the
Irish conflict. Female figures are presented in the poems as ana-
logues for the victims of the conflict and the conflict's source
respectively. As the first section of *North* draws to a close, Heaney
offers a further gendered image of the situation in the poems
'Ocean's Love to Ireland' and 'Act of Union'. The first of these
poems returns us to the early colonial era which we saw Heaney
explore in 'Bog Oak', when he presented us with an image of
Edmund Spenser 'dreaming sunlight' as the starving Irish crept
out of the woods. In 'Ocean's Love to Ireland' Heaney turns to a
contemporary and friend of Spenser's, Walter Ralegh, who, like
Spenser, had extensive colonial interests in Ireland. Heaney's
poem takes as its point of departure both Ralegh's own poetic
fragment 'The Ocean's Love to Cynthia' and an anecdote from
Ralegh's biography concerning his raping of a young woman.
This story is related in the first section of the poem and then,
in the second section, Heaney goes on to make reference to
Ralegh's presence (together with Spenser) at the mass execution
of a small Spanish force which had landed in the south-west
of Ireland. The soldiers were put to death, despite having sur-
rendered to the English (Spenser offers a justification for the
killings in his *View of the Present State of Ireland*). In the third
and final section of the poem, Heaney conflates these sexual and
colonial anecdotes to suggest that Ireland, in its colonial predica-
ment, is in a similar position to the victim of Ralegh's act of rape.

A personified Ireland merges with the figure of the assaulted woman in the final stanza:

> She fades from their somnolent clasp
> Into ringlet-breath and dew,
> The ground possessed and repossessed.

(N. 41)

In 'Act of Union' this metaphorical imagining of Ireland as the victim of English sexual assault is made even more explicit. Where in 'Ocean's Love to Ireland', Heaney describes Ralegh as 'back[ing] the maid to a tree | as Ireland is backed to England' (N. 40), in the second poem of the pair, England is presented as 'the tall kingdom over [Ireland's] shoulder' (N. 43), who penetrates the quiescent, female Ireland, engendering, in the process, the colony of the North. As the metaphorized England tells Ireland: 'His parasitical | And ignorant little fists already | Beat at your borders and I know they're cocked | At me across the water.' The poem gloomily can envision no resolution to the conflict, as England comments in its closing lines:

> No treaty
> I foresee will salve completely your tracked
> And stretchmarked body, the big pain
> That leaves you raw, like opened ground, again.

(N. 43–4)

Despite the delicate aspirations and hopefulness of 'Funeral Rites', then, it is this tone of despair that predominates in *North*, both throughout the mythologizing, historicizing poems of the first section and the more contemporary pieces of the short second section, where *Wintering Out*'s poem of dedication is repeated as the closing section of 'Whatever You Say Say Nothing' and, in 'Orange Drums, Tyrone, 1966', the Protestant drummer beats out an anti-Catholic rhythm that sets the air vibrating:

> To every cocked ear, expert in its greed,
> His battered signature subscribes 'No Pope'.
> The goatskin's sometimes plastered with his blood.
> The air is pounding like a stethoscope.

(N. 62)

This trajectory of despair is registered in the poems placed at the opening and the conclusion of part one of the book. Both poems centre on the mythical conflict between Hercules and Antaeus. Antaeus draws his strength from the land and is renewed by the land every time he touches it. In the first of the two poems he is triumphant and unassailable, never having been defeated. In the second poem, however, he faces a Hercules who 'has the measure | of resistance and black powers | feeding off the territory' (*N*. 46) and who, therefore, raises him off the land and holds him tightly as his strength drains away, finally crushing him to death. In both poems, Antaeus serves as a figure for the native communities who opposed the advance of colonialism throughout the world. The struggle of these traditional, pastoral, earthbound societies was, Heaney suggests, always doomed to failure, as they faced an adversary whose technological advantage and whose world-view always outstripped and exceeded that of the communities who resisted them.

Both these poems register a note of pessimism and exhaustion which resonates with the dominant register of *North*. Its occasional moments of mythically imagined optimism notwithstanding, the volume, taken as a whole, is brooding, distraught, and deeply conflicted. It indicates anxieties and uncertainties which would play themselves out more explicitly in the volumes that succeeded it.

3

'I hear again the sure confusing drum': Reversions and Revisions

In an article on Heaney entitled 'The Trouble with Seamus', James Simmons castigates the poet for offering the reader, in *North*, a 'barren nationalism [that] descends into vanity and self-pity'.[1] Edna Longley, in a more substantial consideration of Heaney's work in *Poetry in the Wars*, provides much the same assessment, and in a chapter of the book entitled 'Poetry and Politics in Northern Ireland' she suggests that 'poetry and politics, like church and state, should be separated. And for the same reasons: mysteries distort the rational processes which ideally prevail in social relations; while ideologies confiscate the poet's special passport to *terra incognita*.'[2]

For Simmons and Longley, Heaney indulges too much in politics, or rather, perhaps, indulges in politics of the wrong kind. Other commentators on Heaney's poems on the Irish conflict – especially those included in *North* – have, however, taken a rather different line. Desmond Fennell, for example, in a belligerent but sometimes insightful pamphlet entitled *Whatever You Say, Say Nothing*, observes of Heaney's poems about the North that they say 'nothing, plainly or figuratively'

> about the war, about any of the three main parties to it, or about the issues at stake. Nor, indeed – quite apart from 'saying' – is anything *suggested* about the war except that it is sad, rooted in history, often ruthless, and connected with the oppression of the poet's people and

sacrifice to the goddess. Of course, in the minds of readers, especially if they are at a distance from the scene, the poems about prehistoric bodies in a Jutland bog, and about particulars of the Northern Ireland war, may fuse together as 'poems about irrational violence'; and that is certainly their collective suggestion. But Heaney says nothing about irrational violence, and all he *suggests* about it, generically, is that it is evil and sad: an insight which we hardly need to read poetry for.[3]

What Fennell is objecting to here is what he perceives as a lack of true political engagement in Heaney's poems. Heaney, he proposes, does not address the particularities of the current political situation, but rather offers us, instead, anodyne observations cloaked in the mythic trappings of pagan ritual. Fennell points here to a critique of Heaney's 'political' poems which is most cogently expressed in the analyses of Ciarán Carson and David Lloyd. Though they come to the poetry from quite different perspectives, what both Carson and Lloyd object to in Heaney's work is what they regard as its dangerous conflation of myth and history, such that, again, the political particularities of the situations Heaney writes about become obscured. Reviewing *North* in the *Honest Ulsterman*, Carson observes (with particular reference to 'Punishment'):

> It is as if he is saying, suffering like this is natural; these things have always happened; they happened then, they happen now, and that is sufficient ground for understanding and absolution. It is as if there never were and never will be any political consequences of such acts; they have been removed to the realm of sex, death and inevitability.[4]

Carson's point here is that in assimilating contemporary political actions – killings, punishments, mutilations – to a mythic past, Heaney in some sense 'naturalizes' these actions, makes them seem somehow inevitable, part of an immemorial, tribal cycle that cannot be broken, or even challenged, and, in the process, Heaney lifts these actions and events out of their actual historical and political context, leaving us no sense of *how* or *why* they have happened. Lacking such an understanding, we cannot see our way to envisioning a solution to the crisis in political or truly social terms. The only kind of solution that is possible within this paradigm is something like that offered in poems such as 'Funeral Rites' or 'Broagh', where communities are brought together in highly aestheticized ideal gestures of reconciliation – united by a trope out of the *Njal's Saga*, or by the ability to pronounce the final phoneme of a local place-name. As David Lloyd observes in ' "Pap for the Dispossessed": Seamus Heaney and the Poetics of Identity' – one of the most penetrating and compelling critiques of Heaney's work – Heaney's typical poetic paradigm serves 'to reduce history to myth, furnishing an aesthetic resolution to conflicts constituted in quite specific historical junctures by rendering disparate events as symbolic moments expressive of an underlying continuity of identity'.[5]

While Carson's and Lloyd's criticisms are perceptive and valid, it should also be noted that Heaney is himself anxiously alert to the problematics of writing poems about the Irish political situation.[6] Much of his poetry is scored with the apprehension that his sense of responsibility as a Northern Irish poet brings to him – a responsibility felt all the more keenly because of Heaney's profound attraction to the work of the Russian poet Osip Mandelstam, who suffered greatly at the hands of the Soviet authorities because of his fidelity to his poetic vision. In the sequence 'A Northern Hoard' in *Wintering Out*, Heaney worries again and again about the issue of whether the poet can ever have any kind of effective role in the face of intense suffering, as he asks himself such questions as 'Why do I unceasingly | arrive late to condone | infected sutures | and ill-knit bone?' (*WO* 30) and 'What do I say if they wheel out their dead?' (*WO* 31). Repeatedly he wonders just what the poet has to offer in circumstances of overwhelming grief and loss.

Heaney's sense of conflict over his own position is clearly focused in 'Exposure', the poem which brings *North* to a close. The title is ironically ambiguous, referring at one and the same time to his celebrity status as a public poet who has received much media exposure and also to his sense of vulnerability (of being 'exposed') as someone who has attempted to engage with the political conflict and who, as a result, bears the weight of his own community's expectations as well as the resentments of some of those in the North who are faithful to an opposing tradition. There may also be a hint in the title of a certain degree of anxiety on Heaney's part that his poems and public life may lead to exposure of another kind – that he may be revealed as being not truly faithful to what he purports to represent or support, or that he may not live up to the expectations of his own community, who would fashion him as a public spokesman of a particular kind – in short, that he may be exposed as a 'fraud'.

The poem begins by locating the poet geographically, as he opens with the line 'It is December in Wicklow' (*N.* 66). County Wicklow is south of Dublin, in the Republic of Ireland. Heaney and his family had moved to a cottage in Glanmore, in Wicklow, in August 1972. Because he was so prominent a public figure, the move was much commented upon, with the Unionist *Protestant Telegraph* rejoicing in the fact that 'the well-known papist propagandist' was on his way to 'his spiritual home in the popish republic'. In an interview with Seamus Deane in the *New York Times Review* some years later, Heaney recalled his own sense of ambivalence about the move: 'Going to the South was perhaps emblematic for me and was certainly so for some of the people I knew. To the Unionists it looked like a betrayal of the Northern thing. Living in the South, I found myself lonelier, imaginatively.'[7]

In the poem itself, Heaney again troubles over the role of the poet and his political responsibilities. Rooted in his mundane rural home he imagines a hero of mythical proportions who might make a stand for his oppressed people, like David challenging Goliath (the sort of gesture that we imagine might be approved of by Desmond Fennell):

> I walk through damp leaves,
> Husks, the spent flukes of autumn,
>
> Imagining a hero
> On some muddy compound,
> His gift like a slingstone
> Whirled for the desperate.

But it is clear to Heaney in the poem that he himself is not the kind of poet who can play the part of such a David and, in any case, in an earlier poem in the collection – 'The Unacknowledged Legislator's Dream' (the title is derived from Shelley's observation that poets are the unacknowledged legislators of the world) – he had interrogated the notion that a poet in the mould of the heroic David could ever offer anything more than a kind of brief and ineffectual display of political bravado. In the poem, the figure of the poet sinks his 'crowbar in a chink ... under the masonry of state and statute' (*N.* 50), but, while his showy gestures of rebellion elicit a cheer from his 'wronged people [in] their cages', he finds himself quickly captured and, imprisoned by the authorities, discovers that he is regarded with a certain indulgent good humour by the agents of the system he has sought to overthrow:

> The commandant motions me to be seated. 'I am
> honoured to add a poet to our list.' He is amused
> and genuine. 'You'll be safer here, anyhow.'

The machinery of state is, finally, untroubled by the poet's grand gesture of insurrection.

Unable or unwilling to fulfil the role of an insurgent David, Heaney in 'Exposure' puzzles over his position as someone who lies outside the easy categorizations of the political realm, as he writes: 'I am neither internee nor informer; | An inner émigré, grown long-haired | And thoughtful' (*N.* 67). He is, in other words, neither a victim of the political situation, an emblematic member of his people ('internees' were suspected militant activists who were imprisoned by the authorities without trial), nor is he a traitor to his people (an 'informer', who betrays members of his own community to the authorities). In a phrase derived from the old Soviet regime (specifically, from the official designation of the imprisoned Mandelstam), he presents himself instead as 'an inner émigré' – someone finally disjoined from the political situation while still being subject to it.

As the poem draws to a conclusion, Heaney offers a further set of images intended to indicate his sense of his own situation, describing himself as 'a wood-kerne'

> Escaped from the massacre,
> Taking protective colouring
> From bole and bark, feeling
> Every wind that blows;
>
> Who, blowing up these sparks
> For their meagre heat, have missed
> The once-in-a-lifetime portent,
> The comet's pulsing rose.

In one sense, these stanzas seem like an appropriate conclusion to *North*, in that they appear to indicate a certain exhaustion with *North*'s greater project of attempting to come to terms with the troubled political situation in Ireland. Having ventured into

the conflict, Heaney at the last imagines himself as a native sol-
dier (a 'wood-kerne') who has managed to escape from the scene
of hostilities, receding into a natural, rural world. To this extent,
the poem seems to signal a kind of 'retreat'.

The closing lines of the poem pick up on an image that Heaney
evokes earlier in the piece, when he writes that

> A comet that was lost
> Should be visible at sunset,
> Those million tons of light
> Like a glimmer of haws and rose-hips,
>
> And I sometimes see a falling star.
> If I could come on meteorite!
>
> (N. 66)

In asserting, at the close of the poem, that he has missed the
'comet's pulsing rose', Heaney may well be ruefully acknowl-
edging a certain sense of having failed, in *North*, adequately to
trace the large-scale outlines of his country's and his commu-
nity's predicament. But there is also, we may feel, a sense in
the poem as a whole that a certain fidelity to the 'meagre heat' of
small-scale particularities is, in itself, both more necessary and
more valid than the kind of large-scale mythic exegesis that he
elsewhere attempts. In this sense, we might say that Heaney
himself discovers within his work the very critique of his poetry
which commentators such as Lloyd and Carson have offered.
As in the case of 'The Unacknowledged Legislator's Dream',
where Heaney queries the effectiveness of ostentatious political/
poetic gestures, here too he seems to question the efficacy of
attempting (as he does in so many of the poems of *North*) to
construct grand political and mythic narratives, whose overarch-
ing trajectory fully accounts for the contemporary conflict.

Such a view of Heaney's position in 'Exposure' suggests that
what he seeks, in Glanmore, is less a retreat from the politi-
cal situation as such than one from what he calls in the
poem 'The diamond absolutes' of easy political certainties and
all-encompassing historical and mythical narratives. Echoing
somewhat the sentiments of Simmons, Carson, and Lloyd,
Maurice Harmon has observed that

> The metaphor of ceremony permeates *North*, a collection deeply
> concerned with the violence of Northern Ireland. The poems do

not confront that violence. They do not speak of individual pain or individual outrage. Instead Heaney adopts a communal response. Whatever personal feelings he has about death and suffering are deflected into large, ceremonial gestures.[8]

If 'Exposure' signals a potential turning-away from such an expansive ceremonial mode, that reorientation is confirmed in the immediate successors to *North* – *Field Work* (1979) and, especially, *Station Island* (1984). In many of the poems in these two volumes Heaney turns precisely to the issue of 'individual pain [and] individual outrage'. Across these volumes he increasingly places under scrutiny the inherited political, cultural, and religious truisms of his community and the dominant register of many of the poems in the two volumes is interrogative. The shift in perception and approach is mirrored in an accompanying shift in poetic form. Where, in *Wintering Out* and *North*, Heaney had adopted the narrow 'artesian stanza' – a form with which he sought, metaphorically, to drill down into the prehistoric sources of conflict – from *Field Work* onwards the poetic line fills out again, expanding to carry the weight of interrogation.

We should note that Heaney does continue to feel a responsibility to speak for his community in these volumes. In *Field Work*'s 'The Toome Road', in particular, he registers a sense of bitterness at the continuing presence of British troops in Northern Ireland. In the poem, he imagines an encounter between a Northern Irish farmer and a British Army convoy, on patrol along a stretch of country road. The farmer asserts his sense of indignation at what he perceives as this foreign intrusion into a landscape in which he is deeply rooted as a native. 'How long were they approaching down my roads | As if they owned them?' he asks, and he goes on to assert his own sense of connection with the land:

> I had rights-of-way, fields, cattle in my keeping,
> Tractors hitched to buckrakes in open sheds,
> Silos, chill gates, wet slates, the greens and reds
> Of outhouse roofs.

> (*FW* 15)

By the end of the poem, the British soldiers are addressed as 'charioteers', thus becoming conflated with their imperial precursors from the Roman Empire. The speaker in the poem offers them a defiant declaration:

> O charioteers, above your dormant guns,
> It stands here still, stands vibrant as you pass,
> The invisible, untoppled omphalos.

The implication is that, just as the Roman Empire has declined and fallen, so too the resources of the local community – the 'omphalos' (a word which Heaney associates with the pumping of water from a communal well – see *Preoccupations*, 17) – will ultimately outlast the colonial regime.

'The Toome Road' seems to suggest that the defeat of colonialism will be effected through the feat of simple endurance. Elsewhere in *Field Work* Heaney engages with the consequences of a more militant form of nationalism and of political violence generally. 'After a Killing', the first section of 'Triptych', was written in the wake of the assassination of Christopher Ewart-Biggs, the British ambassador to Ireland, whose car was blown up by the IRA in 1976. The poem is haunted by the presence, in the first stanza, of two shadowy gunmen:

> There they were, as if our memory hatched them,
> As if the unquiet founders walked again:
> Two young men with rifles on the hill,
> Profane and bracing as their instruments.
>
> (FW 12)

The stanza is curiously ambiguous. Twice in the first two lines we are offered the uncertainty of statements introduced with the words 'as if'. The young men appear 'as if' they have been summoned out of memory (presumably a kind of 'communal memory', since the poem invokes 'we' rather than 'I'); they appear 'as if' they might be the returned spirits of those whose struggle led to the founding of the nation. It is not clear, then, whether Heaney feels that the community is in sympathy with these militants, nor is it clear whether he feels that there is a clear line of continuity between earlier armed struggles and the violent campaign being pursued in contemporary Ireland (the question of whether the contemporary IRA is continuous with the IRA whose 1916 uprising served to break the link with Britain is always a contentious issue in Ireland). The sense of ambiguity is sustained in the closing line of the stanza, where the gunmen are seen as 'profane' and 'bracing'. 'Profane' suggests that they are unholy, polluted, that they engage in acts of defilement and violation. But 'bracing' conjures up images of strength, vigour, and defiance. Similarly, in the concluding line of the stanza, the rifles which the gunmen carry are described as 'instruments' (rather than, for instance, weapons), suggesting precision, craft, and skill rather than violence and murder.

Heaney seems unwilling to surrender his ambivalence over the course of 'Triptych'. In the second section of the poem, 'Sibyl', we are offered powerful images of desecration and its consequences and enjoined to a discipline of pardon and mercy, as when the section's *aisling*-like (dreamlike) figure foresees ineluctable decline for her people unless

> forgiveness finds its nerve and voice,
> Unless the helmeted and bleeding tree
> Can green and open buds like infants' fists
> And the fouled magma incubate
>
> Bright nymphs.

> (FW 13)

At the same time, however, there seems to be an unwillingness on the part of the poet fully to adopt this position in the face of provocation and oppression. The third section of the poem, 'At the Water's Edge', struggles to establish itself in the idyllic natural world of the sacred islands of Northern Ireland's Lough Erne, but the insular tranquillity is troubled by 'the thick rotations | Of an army helicopter patrolling' (FW 14). As in the case of 'The Toome Road', an alien element intrudes itself into the natural landscape. In the final stanza of the poem, the sound of the rotor blades summons up memories of another helicopter, this time hovering over a political protest – a march to mark public outrage at the killing of thirteen unarmed Civil Rights demonstrators by the British Army on 'Bloody Sunday' in January 1972:

> How we crept before we walked! I remembered
> The helicopter shadowing our march at Newry,
> The scared, irrevocable steps.

The march is a sign of defiance in the face of the shadowing helicopter, but we might wonder exactly what it is that Heaney is signalling when he writes 'How we crept before we walked!' What is 'creeping' and what is 'walking'? The tentative steps of the protest march are 'irrevocable': in the wake of the protest there is no going back to an attitude of submissiveness in the face of oppression. But we might ask ourselves, again, whether the defiance of the protest march is continuous with the 'bracing' defiance of the gunmen with whom Heaney opens the poem. Indeed, we might ask whether resistance to oppression is to be seen as running legitimately to the politically motivated killing that provides the occasion for the poem.

Heaney does not address these questions in 'Triptych', but he does in some measure begin to confront them in 'Casualty', another of *Field Work*'s poems to take up the question of the aftermath of the Bloody Sunday killings. The central figure presented in this poem is Louis O'Neill, a Catholic fisherman who was a neighbour and acquaintance of Heaney's in the North. O'Neill was, as the poem puts it, 'blown to bits' in an IRA pub bombing, carried out in reprisal for Bloody Sunday. The IRA had imposed a curfew on the Catholic community, but O'Neill had defied it, searching out an open pub in which to enjoy his usual evening's drinking. Heaney imagines O'Neill at the moment of the explosion

> as he turned
> In that bombed offending place,
> Remorse fused with terror
> In his still knowable face,
> His cornered outfaced stare
> Blinding in the flash.
>
> (*FW* 22–3)

In contrast with 'Triptych', where the victim whose death prompts the poem never appears and is never even evoked, in 'Casualty' we are presented with a vivid image of the victim, both in the course of his life and in the last moment before that life is destroyed. More than this, he is allowed a voice in the poem, as Heaney imagines himself being gently interrogated by the murdered O'Neill:

> How culpable was he
> That night when he broke
> Our tribe's complicity?
> 'Now you're supposed to be
> An educated man,'

> I hear him say. 'Puzzle me
> The right answer to that one.'
>
> (FW 23)

O'Neill's death forces Heaney to confront the deep moral con-
flicts to which the campaign of violence gives rise. He has no
answer to offer O'Neill, but he welcomes the process of inter-
rogation the fisherman provokes, as he addresses O'Neill directly
in the closing lines of the poem: 'Dawn-sniffing revenant, I
Plodder through midnight rain, I Question me again' (FW 24).

Elsewhere in *Field Work*, and subsequently in *Station Island*,
Heaney memorializes other victims of the Northern Irish con-
flict. Unlike the highly mythologized victims of *North*, many
of these figures are presented, like Louis O'Neill, in the full
flow of a life interrupted by an unexpected and brutal death.
'A Postcard from North Antrim' provides a vivid sketch of Sean
Armstrong, a friend of Heaney's from Queen's University, who
had spent some time in a Sausalito commune, but who returned
to Belfast to become involved in social work. In the first three
stanzas Heaney offers Armstrong a selection of good-humoured
postcard images of his own life. When Armstrong's death comes,
in the concluding lines of the fourth stanza, it is unexpected and
shocking:

> You were the clown
> Social worker of the town
> Until your candid forehead stopped
> A pointblank teatime bullet.
>
> (FW 19)

The insertion of the homely 'teatime' between 'pointblank' and
'bullet' serves to render the killing all the more disturbing and
affecting, and, though the second half of the poem returns to
images of social occasions shared with Armstrong, the whole
atmosphere of the poem, as Michael Parker ably indicates,
has been tainted by the brutal murder. Even the wine which
Armstrong freely distributes at the end is reminiscent of his
own spilt blood.[9]

Another victim to be memorialized in *Field Work* is Heaney's
own second cousin Colum McCartney, whose murder by
Protestant gunmen is recalled in 'The Strand at Lough Beg'.

Like much of *Field Work*, this poem is greatly indebted to the work of Dante, especially his *Divine Comedy*. The poem opens with an epigraph from the *Purgatorio* and ends with an image which is also borrowed from the same source. In Dante's poem, Virgil, the poet's guide, washes the grime of Hell from off the poet's face before he moves on to the next stage of his journey and enters Purgatory: 'When we were at a part where the dew resists the sun and, being in the shade, is little dispersed, my Master gently laid both hands outspread on the grass. I, there-fore, aware of his purpose, reached toward him my tear-stained cheeks and on them he wholly restored that colour which Hell had hidden in me.'[10] Heaney conceives of performing the same ritual of purification on the body of his murdered cousin, as he pictures himself finding McCartney 'With blood and roadside muck in [his] hair and eyes' (*FW* 18). Heaney imagines himself

> kneel . . . in brimming grass
> And gather up cold handfuls of the dew
> To wash you, cousin. I dab you clean with moss
> Fine as the drizzle out of a low cloud.

At the end of the purification ritual in the *Purgatorio*, Virgil girds the poet with rushes which 'spring up again immediately in the place where he had plucked' them. Likewise, Heaney plaits 'green scapulars' for his cousin from 'rushes that shoot green again'. The poem ends, then, with images of purification and renewal.

In some respects we might feel that 'The Strand at Lough Beg' has more in common with the mythologizing poems of *North* than it has with its companion pieces on political violence in *Field Work*. We might recall, for instance, the image of the mur-dered woman in 'Punishment', her body metaphorized into an aesthetic object, as the wind 'blows her nipples | to amber beads' (*N.* 30). Similarly the consolation offered here – like the conso-lations and reconciliations offered in *North* – is metaphorical and highly mythologized. Heaney himself picks up on this very issue when he returns to consider McCartney's death once more in *Station Island*, a volume more searching and more sceptical than its immediate predecessor. In section VIII of the collec-tion's title poem, McCartney, like Louis O'Neill in 'Casualty', is granted a voice to question the poet. As he first encounters the 'bleeding, pale-faced boy, plastered in mud' (*SI* 82), the poet is unable immediately to recognize him, and McCartney sharply prompts his memory by reminding him of where he was – at Jerpoint Abbey, Kilkenny, in the south of Ireland – on the day when his cousin was murdered:

> You were there with poets when you got the word
> and stayed there with them, while your own flesh and blood
> was carted to Bellaghy from the Fews.
> They showed more agitation at the news
> than you did.

The poet attempts to defend himself for pledging a greater fidelity to the world of poetry than to the actuality of his cousin's death. As part of his defence, he offers McCartney an aesthetic image and a metaphor for his own reaction: 'I kept seeing a grey stretch of Lough Beg | and the strand empty at daybreak. | I felt like the bottom of a dried-up lake' (*SI* 83). On hearing this, McCartney presses home his attack – it is precisely this metaphorizing tendency, which leads away from the particular to the aesthetic, that he objects to in Heaney's handling of his death in 'The Strand at Lough Beg':

> 'You saw that, and you wrote that – not the fact,
> You confused evasion and artistic tact.
> The Protestant who shot me through the head
> I accuse directly, but indirectly, you
>
> .   .   .   .
>
> ... you whitewashed ugliness and drew
> the lovely blinds of the *Purgatorio*
> and saccharined my death with morning dew.'

Again like Louis O'Neill, the figure of McCartney here forces Heaney to reconsider his allegiances and responsibilities as a poet. The section of 'Station Island' dedicated to McCartney is typical of the sequence as a whole, which is very much concerned with issues of reappraisal and reassessment and with the interrogation of old beliefs and fidelities.

'Station Island' takes its basic conceit from the tradition of pilgrimage literature associated with an island in Lough Derg in County Donegal. The island itself has strong associations with Saint Patrick, and the pilgrimage involves a three-day stay, during which time the pilgrim fasts and prays, in addition to completing, barefoot, nine circuits of the island. A number of Irish authors have written about the pilgrimage experience and Heaney fits his own narrative within that literary tradition.

In 'Station Island' Heaney comes face to face with the ideologies of his community and reassesses his own position in relation to them. As in the case of *Field Work*, Heaney is greatly indebted to Dante and, like the *Divine Comedy*, 'Station Island' is structured as a series of encounters with the ghosts of dead figures who are either known to Heaney personally or have been important to him as a writer. The first two encounters take place before the poet arrives on the island itself and the final encounter also occurs on the mainland, as he steps off the boat returning him from the island.

In the first of the encounters, the poet comes upon an old County Derry neighbour, Simon Sweeney, who had troubled Heaney as a child and who returns now to disturb him again. Sweeney appears in the poet's childhood as a transgressive figure, upon whom the child projects his fears of the alien and the unknown. Sweeney tells him:

> When they bade you listen
> in the bedroom dark
> to wind and rain in the trees
> and think of tinkers camped
> under a heeled-up cart
>
> you shut your eyes and saw
> a wet axle and spokes
> in moonlight, and me
> streaming from the shower,
> headed for your door.
>
> (*SI* 62)

The specific nature of Sweeney's deviance, which marks him as an alien and transgressive presence, is registered by the poet when he first recognizes his old neighbour. 'I know you, Simon Sweeney,' he says, 'for an old Sabbath-breaker | who has been dead for years' (*SI* 61). Sweeney stands outside the community because he transgresses its Christian injunction against working on Sunday – the Sabbath Day, traditionally dedicated to rest and religious contemplation. Sweeney's response to the poet's remembered piety has a double force to it, as he tells the poet

'Damn all you know'. On the one hand, Sweeney is condemning Heaney for his presumptuousness, indicating that, in his uninformed ignorance, he knows nothing ('damn all'). On the other hand, his riposte runs deeper than this, as he also condemns (damns) all of the knowledge, all of the traditional pieties, that the poet has accepted on faith for so many years.

Sweeney provides the first signal of an interrogation of Heaney's religious sense of self which runs through the poem as a whole and which finds focus again in section IV, where the poet encounters another neighbour, Terry Keenan. Keenan had joined the priesthood as an adolescent and served on the missions in South America, proselytising for the Roman Catholic faith. He died when his health was broken by the alien climate and conditions. The poet, in addressing Keenan, sees his priestly vocation as a futile surrender to convention, with the young man 'doomed to the decent thing' (SI 70). In the poet's eyes, Keenan is virtually sacrificed to the common pieties of his community:

> Something in them would be ratified
> when they saw you at the door in your black suit,
> arriving like some sort of holy mascot.
>
> You gave too much relief, you raised a siege
> the world had laid against their kitchen grottoes
> hung with holy pictures.

But, again, like Simon Sweeney, Keenan responds forcefully to the poet's easy self-assurance and turns to interrogating the poet's own sense of self. 'What are you doing, going through these motions?' he asks, 'Unless you are here taking the last look' (SI 71). Keenan's question penetrates to the heart of 'Station Island' and he effectively queries what the nature and purpose of Heaney's pilgrimage are. As Neil Corcoran has observed, what the poem presents us with is a peculiarly ironic, even reversed, form of pilgrimage, which 'leads to no confirmation in the religion and values of the tribe, but to something very like a renunciation of them'.[11]

The issue of Heaney's relationship to his sense of religous faith is brought to a head in section XI of the poem, when Heaney recalls another local priest, who had returned to the North from Spain and who, administering confession to Heaney, had once set him the penance of translating into English 'something by Juan de la Cruz' (*SI* 89) – the Spanish mystic, St John of the Cross. Heaney offers his translation as the balance of section XI of the poem. The prayer translated is a profession of faith in religious conviction, in the face of a crisis of belief. Faith is figured in the poem as an 'eternal fountain' which 'call[s] out to every creature' (*SI* 90). The prayer insists throughout on the validity of such beautiful and pure images of faith, despite the fact that the writer is, at the time of writing, uncertain of his beliefs. His crisis is insistently registered by the refrain which completes each stanza with the phrase 'although it is the night'. In the context of the other interrogations of religious belief which we find taking place in 'Station Island', we might feel that, in being imported into Heaney's poem, what happens to St John's prayer is that the balance of the individual stanzas shifts from the profession of faith to the confession of crisis. Within this context, the prayer seems less an articulation of consolation than an acknowledgement of a certain failure of belief.

This same reaction to orthodox religious doctrine can be discerned elsewhere in *Station Island*, especially in a poem such as 'In Illo Tempore', where Heaney again recalls his experiences of religion in childhood. Remembering his attendance at church services, he recollects how 'The big missal splayed | and dangled silky ribbons | of emerald and purple and watery white' (*SI* 118). This leads him on to recall the passive, unquestioning attitude which religion inculcated in the community, as he observes: 'Intransitively we would assist, | confess, receive. The verbs | assumed us. We adored.' This religion leaves no room for independence of thought or action.

We have been tracing Heaney's questioning of traditional religious orthodoxies through from the opening section of 'Station Island'. The second poem in the sequence sets in train another line of interrogation, already familiar to us from our consideration of *Field Work*. In this section, Heaney encounters the nineteenth-century Irish writer William Carleton, who published his own account of the Station Island ritual as *The Lough Derg Pilgrim*. Carleton renounced Catholicism and denounced the pilgrimage tradition as an act of unthinking superstition. As he appears in the poem, he is fully aware of the political implications of rejecting his Catholic identity and deriding it in print:

> hard-mouthed Ribbonmen and Orange bigots
> made me into the old fork-tongued turncoat
> who mucked the byre of their politics.
>
> If times were hard, I could be hard too.
> I made the traitor in me sink the knife.
>
> (*SI* 65)

It is his distaste for stagnant political orthodoxies of all kinds, whether Catholic (in the form of the militant 'Ribbonmen') or Protestant (the 'Orange bigots'), that leads Carleton to reject the pieties of his own community. His hard-edged self-positioning prompts Heaney to attempt to justify what we have already noted as his own habitual political ambiguities. He explains to Carleton that the militancy that he (Carleton) had grown up with had declined, in the community of Heaney's childhood, to the meaningless formalism of an empty subservient and pietistic nationalism:

> 'I have no mettle for the angry role,'
> I said. 'I come from County Derry,
> born in earshot of an Hibernian hall
>
> where a band of Ribbonmen played hymns to Mary.
> By then the brotherhood was a frail procession
> staggering home drunk on Patrick's Day.[']

This compromised, complacent background notwithstanding, however, Heaney is forced in later sections of 'Station Island' to confront the justifications and consequences that violent political actions imply. In the middle segment of the poem he encounters three young men whose deaths have resulted from the political situation. One is his cousin, Colum McCartney, the significance of whose presence in the poem we have already considered; a second is William Strathern, another acquaintance who, like Sean Armstrong, was murdered by Protestant gunmen in a random sectarian killing. Much in the manner of 'A Postcard from North Antrim', Heaney imagines the immediate particulars of Strathern's life – lying in bed beside his wife – as the killers arrive at his door. As he had done in his encounter with Carleton, Heaney finds himself attempting to justify his own political and poetic ambiguities to Strathern: ' "Forgive the way I have lived indifferent – I forgive my timid circumspect involvement," I I I surprised myself by saying' (*SI* 80).

Strathern's response is direct and chilling: ' "Forgive | my eye," he said, "That's all above my head." ' Like Armstrong, Strathern had been shot in the head by his killers, so that his riposte to Heaney not only dismisses the poet's attempt in some measure to justify himself, but, in fact, brings that gesture of self-justification into confrontation with the brutal reality of his own violent death.

What Heaney demonstrates throughout 'Station Island' is that there are no simple ways of engaging with the Northern Irish situation. This point is underlined by his imagined encounter in the poem with a third young man whose death was connected with the political situation. In section IX, the poet believes he hears the voice of a prisoner who starved himself to death in jail. It is likely that Heaney has in mind here Francis Hughes, a Bellaghy neighbour who was imprisoned for IRA activities and who took part in the hunger strikes of 1980–1, when nationalist prisoners refused food in protest over the government's decision to reclassify them as 'criminals' rather than as 'political prisoners'.[12] In all, ten men lost their lives; Hughes was the second of the group to die.

Where the apparent ambiguity in the face of violent political action which we witnessed in the opening section of 'Triptych' would appear in large measure to have been driven out of Heaney's poetry by his engaging with the consequences of such violence, what persists here in this section of 'Station Island' is a sense of the poet's responsibility to act in some way in the face of provocation and oppression (an issue which, we will recall, engages Heaney in the final section of 'Triptych'). The issue which lay at the centre of the hunger strikes dispute has a particular force for Heaney, in that, in seeking to criminalize nationalist (and loyalist) prisoners, the government was denying that their actions were politically motivated and had been undertaken as a response to the political crisis. This raises for Heaney, again, the question of what kind of response to the situation is appropriate and adequate. Though he does not condone Hughes's violent actions, he nevertheless recognizes them as one kind of response to the contemporary crisis (a recognition refused by the government). This prompts him once again to call himself to task for the inadequacy of his own response, as he cries: 'I repent | My unweaned life that kept me competent | To sleepwalk with connivance and mistrust' and 'I hate how quick I was to know my place. I I hate where I was born, hate everything I That made me biddable and unforthcoming' (*SI* 85).

It is, finally, the figure of James Joyce who releases Heaney from this sense of failed responsibility and inadequate responsiveness which surfaces again and again in 'Station Island'. It is Joyce's hand which 'stretche[s] down from the jetty' (*SI* 92) in the final section of the poem, as Heaney returns to the mainland at the end of his pilgrimage. Joyce, the *émigré* writer who left Ireland for Paris, dismisses Heaney's 'peasant pilgrimage' as an irrelevant waste of time and has little patience for his sense of inadequacy and penitence: 'don't be so earnest,' he cautions him, 'let others wear the sackcloth and the ashes' (*SI* 93). Joyce sets out for Heaney a programme for proceeding in his career as a poet, exhorting him to 'Cultivate a work-lust' and telling him that 'The main thing is to write I for the joy of it' – as Joyce himself did in playfully dismantling and refashioning the English language itself in *Finnegans Wake*. He further advises Heaney:

> Keep at a tangent.
> When they make the circle wide, it's time to swim
>
> out on your own and fill the element
> with signatures on your own frequency,
> echo soundings, searches, probes, allurements,
>
> elver-gleams in the dark of the whole sea.
>
> (*SI* 93–4)

Heaney's Joyce here proposes a view of literature which detaches it from the necessity to provide a direct engagement with the particularities of the immediate political situation. In one sense, this might well be interpreted as a kind of 'cop out' on Heaney's part. If critics like Fennell, Carson, and Lloyd call Heaney to task for failing adequately to respond to the immediate political moment (and if Heaney himself, in some measure, seems to agree with this critique), this closing section of 'Station Island' might well be taken as Heaney's abandonment of the political in the face of his own failure. Such a view of the situation would not be entirely unjustified. Looking back over the span of Heaney's poems on the Irish crisis, we might feel that the poet seems finally to offer us little enough by way of a productive engagement with that crisis. When Heaney published *Station Island* a decade on from his fanciful image of reconciliation in 'Funeral Rites', the list of the dead had increased, as had the sense of bitterness and rancour on all sides in the dispute. Likewise, Heaney's learned disquisitions on Viking lore, archaeology, and etymology have always seemed terribly esoteric and far removed from the lives of those who have borne most in the conflict – the working-class families in Ireland and Britain from whom the majority of the combatants (nationalist and loyalist militants, British soldiers) and casualties are drawn.

This being said, however, it must also be noted that what characterizes Heaney's poems on the political situation is a deep sense of honest striving towards some kind of meaningful encounter with the history and politics of his native country. If he does fail in this attempt, perhaps that failure is more a testament to the complexity of the situation than to his attempts to bend his poetic responsibility towards it. Heaney is one of a large number of writers who have turned their attention to the subject of Northern Ireland in recent years. Much of this writing has been glibly and ignorantly exploitative of the conflict; Heaney ranks as one of a handful of writers (including Brian Friel, Frank McGuinness, Paul Muldoon, and Ciarán Carson) who have genuinely struggled to bring their writing into some kind of fruitful relationship with the contemporary political situation and its historical antecedants.

Joyce's advice to Heaney to turn away from immediate political concerns would appear to be confirmed by a later poem in *Station Island* – 'The Old Icons' – in which Heaney appears finally to disengage himself from the kind of traditional nationalist orthodoxies and pieties to which he had, for much of his life, pledged a kind of wavering allegiance. We should note, however, that the turn away from Irish politics does not signal the advent of an apolitical Heaney. If anything, it indicates a broadening of his political canvas. From *Station Island* onwards, Heaney's political concerns become more wide-ranging, as evidenced by the inclusion of poems such as 'From the Land of the Unspoken' and 'From the Republic of Conscience' in *Seeing Things* (the latter poem having been first published as an Amnesty International pamphlet on Human Rights Day in 1985). This broadening of political interest is also registered in the amount of space dedicated to poets from Eastern Europe in *The Government of the Tongue*. In addition to this widening of his political interests, Heaney also broadens his poetic vision in other ways in the successor volumes to *Station Island*.

4

'It was marvellous and actual': Familiarity and Fantasy

Seamus Heaney once noted in an interview that, sometime after *North* was published, he wrote to the playwright Brian Friel, observing of his poetic practice that he 'no longer wanted a door into the dark'. 'I wanted a door into the light,' he observed, 'to be able to use the first person singular to mean *me* and my life-time.'[1] In the previous chapter we dwelt almost exclusively on the politically informed poetry which Heaney continued to write after *North*, but we should note that, from *Field Work* onwards, Heaney does begin to reintroduce into his work a kind of poetry that is less immediately political, a poetry more rooted in the world of personal concerns. Indeed, viewed in this light, we can see *Field Work* itself as falling very roughly into two halves. In the first stretch of the collection, Heaney continues to struggle with public themes, pursuing further the debates which he initiated in *North*, but, in the second, he turns to contemplate more intimate, more personal concerns.

In part this transition between the two halves of the volume (and, we might say, between the middle phase of Heaney's career and his more recent departures) is mediated through the sequence of poems that lies at the heart of *Field Work* – the 'Glanmore Sonnets'. We have already seen the significance of Glanmore for Heaney in our examination of *North*'s 'Exposure'. In that poem, Glanmore serves as a site of conflict. On the one hand, Heaney's removal to the rural south of Ireland, far distant from the day-to-day experience of the Northern troubles, prompts him to re-evaluate the exact nature of his political commitments

69

as a poet. But, on the other hand, it also provokes a certain sense of anxiety and guilt about his abandonment of his home territory in a time of political crisis. In the 'Glanmore Sonnets', by contrast, Heaney celebrates his family's stint of living in County Wicklow with a kind of ease and freedom that 'Exposure' signally lacks.

In part this celebration marks something of a return for Heaney to the concerns of his early poetry, in which he sought an easy engagement with the particulars of the immediate, natural world. We might note, indeed, that the sonnet sequence opens with several images which will be familiar to us from Heaney's earliest work. The first and second of the Glanmore poems offer the task of ploughing as an image of the poetic act. '[A]rt', he tells us in sonnet I, could be 'a paradigm of earth new from the lathe I Of ploughs' (*FW* 33) and, in sonnet II, he recurs to the image we first saw him deploy in *Death of a Naturalist*'s 'Follower', when he sees the act of turning lines of verse as being analogous to the turning of the plough from one furrow into another: 'Vowels ploughed into other, opened ground, I Each verse returning like the plough turned round' (*FW* 34).

In addition to deploying an imagery which echoes that of his earliest work, Heaney also offers here a sense of the nature of the poetic act which has much in common with his earlier sense of poetry. In sonnet II, he compares the poet's work to that of the sculptor, as, much in the manner of such early poems as 'The Diviner', 'The Forge', and 'Thatcher', he sees both figures as artisans who seek to draw from their mundane raw material an aesthetic form which lies naturally within it:

> 'These things are not secrets but mysteries,'
> Oisin Kelly told me years ago
> In Belfast, hankering after stone
> That connived with the chisel, as if the grain
> Remembered what the mallet tapped to know.

Throughout the 'Glanmore Sonnets' Heaney closely engages once more with the particulars of his immediate surroundings, seeking significances within them, just as his friend Oisin Kelly has sought the contours of his finished sculpture within the block of raw stone he worked upon. In sonnet III, Heaney finds the natural world offering a kind of poetry of its own to him, as he writes:

70

> This evening the cuckoo and the corncrake
> (So much, too much) consorted at twilight.
> It was all crepuscular and iambic.

and

> Outside a rustling and twig-combing breeze
> Refreshes and relents. Is cadences.

(FW 35)

In each case, the world around the poet organizes itself into natural poetic rhythms – 'iambs' and 'cadences'.

In the seventh poem in the sequence, Heaney once again finds himself drawn to the particularities of place-names, as he recalls those names included as a kind of ritual in the gale-warnings routinely broadcast on the radio: 'Dogger, Rockall, Malin, Irish Sea' and 'Minches, Cromarty, The Faroes' (*FW* 39). One particular gale drives a group of French trawlers into a nearby Wicklow harbour and Heaney savours 'their bright names': '*L'Etoile, Le Guillemot, La Belle Hélène*'. The unexpected sight of these exotic, foreign intrusions into the world of the local and the quotidian prompts the poet to an observation which will prove central to much of his later poetry. 'It was marvellous I And actual', he writes, stressing in equal measure the wondrous quality of the experience and its concreteness – the experience is at one and the same time extraordinary and firmly rooted in the material world (their exotic names notwithstanding, these are not the mythical long-boats that we find arising out of a Viking past in Heaney's earlier poetry, but rather ordinary French fishing vessels).

We will return to Heaney's sense of the relationship between the marvellous and the actual later in this chapter. But, first, we might note that, just as he celebrates the actual as providing a kind of access to the marvellous, so too, in the 'Glanmore Sonnets', he celebrates the deep significance of the domestic and the intimate. The figure of the poet's wife is several times invoked in these poems. In sonnet III, she appears in order to puncture his inflated sense of his own life as a poet. In eulogizing their rural existence, he begins to draw a parallel between their lives in Glanmore and Dorothy and William Wordsworth's life together in 'Dove Cottage' in Grasmere, in the English Lake District. His wife, refusing the connection, cuts across him: 'She interrupts: I "You're not going to compare us two . . ."' Later in the volume, in 'An Afterwards', she again performs the same

71

deflationary role, when Heaney imagines her as a kind of female Dante, encountering him on her rounds of the Inferno. Telling him that she has 'closed [her] widowed ears | To the sulphurous news of poets and poetry' (FW 44), she offers, in the closing lines of the poem, a slyly humourous assessment of her husband's life:

> 'You weren't the worst. You aspired to a kind,
> Indifferent, faults-on-both-sides tact.
> You left us first, and then those books, behind.'

Elsewhere in the 'Glanmore Sonnets', the poet's wife serves as a point of intimate, human contact which offers a bulwark against terror and anguish. In sonnet VIII, the poet's mind fills with images of the aftermath of bloody conflict – 'I thought of dew on armour and carrion. | What would I meet, bloodboltered, on the road?' (FW 40) – and with unspecified fears of the kind he once registered in a poem such as 'The Barn' – 'How deep into the woodpile sat the toad? | What welters through this dark hush on the crops?' The poem then shifts to an image of an old woman, comforting a Down's Syndrome child, a shared memory of a trip made with his wife. In the closing couplet of the poem, the poet turns to his spouse, urgently seeking sexual relief from these accumulated fears and anxieties: 'Come to me quick, I am upstairs shaking. | My all of you birchwood in lightning.'

In our analysis of *Death of a Naturalist*, we noted the clutch of marriage poems which Heaney includes in the closing section of his first collection. *Field Work* includes a similar group, not so much of marriage poems, as of poems concerning sexual intimacy. The 'Glanmore Sonnets' end, for instance, with a delicate evocation of the first sexual encounter between the poet and his wife. The context of the recollection is a dream in which he imagines the two of them as a pair of eloping lovers, in the manner of *The Merchant of Venice*'s Lorenzo and Jessica, or Diarmuid and Grainne from the traditional Irish story *Toríacht Diarmuida agus Grainne*. Switching from the mythical to the remembered, he writes:

> And in that dream I dreamt – how like you this? –
> Our first night years ago in that hotel
> When you came with your deliberate kiss
> To raise us towards that lovely and painful
> Covenants of flesh; our separateness;
> The respite in our dewy dreaming faces.

> (FW 42)

As so often in Heaney, the poem offers us a point of reference derived from the English Renaissance. The line 'how like you this?' is taken from Sir Thomas Wyatt's poem 'They fle from me that sometyme did me seke', in which the poet's lover, coming to him in the night and letting 'her lose gowne from her shoulders . . . fall', asks him 'dere hert, howe like you this?'[2] In Wyatt's poem, this sexual encounter is remembered with a certain degree of bitterness, as an instance of the pleasure now being denied him in his isolation, since 'all is torned . . . | Into a straunge fasshion for forsaking'. In Heaney's poem, by contrast, the moment of bold intimacy is presented, not as an episode recollected from a lost world, but, rather, in a complex sense, as a point of initiation. It is both a sexual initiation (a kind of 'initiation rite') and also the initiation into their lives together as partners.

The persistence of a certain kind of quiet longing and sexual intimacy is registered elsewhere in *Field Work* also, especially in such poems as 'The Otter', 'The Skunk', and sections of the title poem, 'Field Work', itself. In these poems Heaney offers tender images of a life of shared physical intimacies. Sometimes, as in 'The Skunk', these images are charged with a certain kind of comic incongruity, as the poet compares his wife – in her 'head-down, tail-up hunt in a bottom drawer | For the black plunge-line nightdress' (*FW* 48) – to a skunk he once saw in California. The humour of the comparison, in contrast with the raw sexual desire of a poem such as the eighth Glanmore sonnet, indicates the easy intimacy of a long-term, settled relationship.

The engagement with the intimate, the domestic, and the familial, which Heaney re-initiates in *Field Work*, continues in its successor volume, *Station Island*. In 'The Underground', the opening poem of the collection, Heaney again recollects the earliest days of his marriage, as he recalls a trip to a Proms concert at London's Albert Hall during his honeymoon. Heaney's children also appear at several points in this volume, with the poet explicitly dedicating two poems to them – 'A Hazel Stick for Catherine Ann' and 'A Kite for Michael and Christopher'. What the poems in which the children appear seem to offer is, again, a kind of initiation process, except that, now, it is the poet's offspring who are being initiated into the world of resonant particularities – the world from which much of Heaney's poetry is derived. In 'Changes' the poet leads one of his children to an old pump (an image always charged with heavy significance in Heaney's work) and they share together the unexpected pleasure of discovering a bird and her egg nestled in its disused spout. In closing, the poet exhorts his child to

> 'Remember this.
> It will be good for you to retrace this path
>
> when you have grown away and stand at last
> at the very centre of the empty city.'
>
> (*SI* 37)

The gesture is strikingly reminiscent of numerous moments in another poet much concerned with childhood, William Wordsworth, especially his observation in 'Tintern Abbey' that the 'beauteous forms' which he has experienced in the country-side near the abbey have often come back to him 'in lonely rooms, and 'mid the din I Of towns and cities', affording him

> sensations sweet,
> Felt in the blood, and felt along the heart;
> And passing even into my purer mind,
> With tranquil restoration.[3]

What both Wordsworth and Heaney suggest is that what the rural experience, the intimate contact with nature, provides is a resource which can be drawn upon in other times and other circumstances.

In the two poems specifically titled for Heaney's children, we find, again, attention afforded to a particular object or experience which indicates significances beyond its immediate import. 'A Hazel Stick for Catherine Ann' memorializes a simple object – a hazel wand cut for the child by her father. In the child's hands, however, the stick is turned to a variety of uses. The imagination which plays upon the stick is emblematized by the glow-worm, which the child encounters for the first time ever on the same evening as her father trims the wand for her. In the closing lines of the poem, the insect and the stick are brought together, as the glow-worm's light brightens 'the eye I in the blunt cut end' of the stick (*SI* 43). What the stick gives access to, we might say, is a world of vision and illumination. 'A Kite for Michael and Christopher' traces a similar trajectory. The soaring of the kite seems to indicate a kind of transcendence of the material world. The poem closes on an unexpected note, however, as the poet signals to his children just what connection the kite affords:

> take it in your two hands, boys, and feel
> the strumming, rooted, long-tailed pull of grief.
> You were born fit for it.
> Stand in here in front of me
> and take the strain.
>
> (*SI* 44)

What the soaring kite offers is not an escape from the world, but a profound connection with the anguish of life – the 'long-tailed pull of grief'. That the poet should summon his children to experience this connection is indicative of the capacity of the kite to mediate the encounter, to make it possible for them to 'take the strain'. The kite provides, thus, not a point of exit from the world of 'gravity', but a point of fruitful and meaningful engagement with that world.

What Heaney sets out in 'A Kite for Michael and Christopher' is, as much as anything else, an aesthetic or poetic creed, and we can see the kite as a figure for the creative act. We will notice that a common thread links a poem such as 'Glanmore Sonnets' VII, where the actual and the marvellous are deeply intertwined, and 'A Kite for Michael and Christopher', where the marvellous (in the form of the soaring kite) facilitates a productive encountering of the actual. Before we turn to explore the implications of these ideas for the general thrust of Heaney's later poetry, we might first consider a further set of poems in which Heaney again engages with the domestic and the familial. These are the poems in *The Haw Lantern* and *Seeing Things*, where Heaney attempts to come to terms with his relationship with his parents.

Heaney's mother died in the autumn of 1984, his father two years later. In *The Haw Lantern* the poet meditates upon the first of these parental deaths in a sequence entitled 'Clearances'. In the second of these poems he offers a slightly whimsical image of his mother's afterlife, as she arrives back after her death to a kind of celestial version of her own parental home. Her dead father welcomes her 'With spectacles pushed back on a clean bald head' (*HL* 26) and she re-enters a familiar meticulous and

precise world: 'The kettle whistled. Sandwich and teascone |
Were present and correct.' The attention to detail here, some-
what comic in the context of traditional notions of the afterlife,
is characteristic of the sequence as a whole. Indeed, it is only
through an engagement with the details of a common – in the
sense both of 'shared' and of 'everyday' – life that Heaney is
able to come to terms with his mother's death. What he recalls
of his life with his mother – and what enables him to recon-
cile himself to her passing – is a series of concrete tasks which
they shared together. In the third poem in the sequence, for
instance, he recollects times he spent with her on Sunday morn-
ings peeling potatoes, while the rest of the family were at church.
This simple task constitutes for Heaney a kind of intimacy which
has a significance far outstripping surface appearances. Indeed,
it is the image of this unspoken intimacy which returns to the
poet's mind and consoles him far more than prayer does at
the point of his mother's death. While the priest, he tells us,
was intoning the prayers for the dying,

> And some were responding and some crying
> I remembered her head bent towards my head,
> Her breath in mine, our fluent dipping knives –
> Never closer the whole rest of our lives.

(HL 27)

We are offered an image of a similar kind of intimacy in the
fifth poem in the sequence, where Heaney remembers perform-
ing another domestic chore with his mother – folding sheets
together as they took them off the clothes line. Again, the
routine, formal rhythms of the task provide a kind of structure
within which their unspoken and unacknowledged connection
can find a place:

> . . . we'd stretch and fold and end up hand to hand
> For a split second as if nothing had happened
> For nothing had that had not always happened
> Beforehand, day by day, just touch and go,
> Coming close again by holding back.

(HL 29)

The poem speaks both of a failure of true intimacy, a stultifying
lack of real communication, and also of the way in which such

communication can be (and must be) channelled into alternative modes of expression. The faint touchings of the customary routine of the domestic chore become a means whereby mother and son can make contact – however fleeting – with each other.

In the fourth of the 'Clearances' poems, Heaney returns to a topic which was a significant concern of his in *Death of a Naturalist*: the sense of alienation from his family that he felt as he had grown away from them educationally and culturally. In 'Clearances' he registers how, with his mother, he effected a kind of compromise, in an attempt to bridge the gap between them. In her company, he tells us, he would change his way of speaking, switching from his acquired, educated register to the manner of speech which was native to him: 'I'd *naw* and *aye* | And decently relapse into the wrong | Grammar' (*HL* 28). The effect of the compromise is to keep mother and son 'allied and at bay' and, again, we get a sense of a balance being struck between a certain failure of communication, on the one hand, and the effecting of that communication through alternative channels, on the other.

If Heaney manages to come to terms with his relationship with his mother in *Haw Lantern*'s 'Clearances', in *Seeing Things* he attempts to work through his relationship with his father – a relationship which, we will recall from a poem such as *Death of a Naturalist*'s 'Follower', is altogether more vexed. In 'Man and Boy' the poet effects a connection with his father by telescoping three generations of fathers and sons. His access to his own father's death is ventured through his father's experience of *his* father's death, as he ran through the fields to tell him that the mower (with his scythe, a figure for death in the poem) had finished his work. The poet combines this vision of the past with a vision of the future, as he imagines himself in old age piggybacked 'Like a witless elder rescued from the fire' (*ST* 15). Heaney is alluding here to the story of Virgil's *Aeneid*, in which Aeneas carries his father Anchises from the ruins of Troy, following the fall of the city. In Heaney's version of the filial myth, however, it is he himself as son turned old man who will be carried away, not by one of his own sons, but rather by a youthful incarnation of his father. What we get here, then, is a collapsing of male generations into a kind of equivalence, as a relationship of equality, interchangeability, and continuity is established among the various fathers and sons who figure in the poem.

A similar resolution to the generational struggle between fathers and sons is effected in a further pair of poems in *Seeing Things*: 'The Ash Plant' and the immediately succeeding 'I.I.87'. In the first of these poems, Heaney offers a picture of his father in his last days, lying in bed, inactive, the world continuing with its routines without him. As his father dies away from the world, one last spark of habit prompts him to reach out for his 'ash plant' – the stick which he regularly carried about with him on his rounds of the family farm. The action of connecting with the stick has the effect of steadying the dying man and affording him a sense of location:

> his wasting hand
> Gropes desperately and finds the phantom limb
> Of an ash plant in his grasp, which steadies him.
> Now he has found his touch he can stand his ground.
>
> (*ST* 19)

In the short, three-line poem which immediately follows 'The Ash Plant', Heaney extends the connection from his father to himself:

> Dangerous pavements.
> But I face the ice this year
> With my father's stick.
>
> (*ST* 20)

Now that his father is dead, he has acquired as an inheritance his father's stick, and he too feels steadied and located with it in his possession. The conflicts which he experienced with his father have been dissolved by his parent's death and he is able to come to terms both with the death itself and with the psychological inheritance which his father has bequeathed to him through the symbolic possession of his father's stick. We might note a rather obvious psycho-sexual connection here, in that the acquisition of the phallic object of the stick may be emblematic, at a sexual level, of the final resolution of a kind of oedipal struggle between son and father. In more general terms, we can say that possessing this tangible marker of continuity with his lost parent serves to steady the poet within the

uncertainties of his own life – the 'ice' which he must nego-
tiate. Blake Morrison, who wrote the first book-length study of
Heaney, delineates a similar symbolic moment of filial posses-
sion to Heaney's in his memoir of his own parent's death,
And When Did You Last See Your Father? As he prepares for his
father's funeral, he writes: 'I put on his white nylon shirt, black
tie, grey suit, black woollen socks, black shoes. I am going to
his funeral in his clothes' and, again, at the funeral itself: 'I stand
in his clothes – how well they fit me now – gazing down at the
earth. Snow blows across his black scuffed shoes, the bottom of
his greatcoat, his trouser turn-ups.'[4]

The ash plant in these poems figures as a kind of symbolic
object that provides access not to a realm which transcends the
everyday material world, but rather to one which facilitates a
productive engagement with that world. In the hand of the dying
man, cut off from the realm of his customary routines, it offers
a sense of connectedness and location; after his death, in the
hands of his son, it offers a different sense of connectedness,
allowing the son more easily to negotiate the uncertainties of
the world he inhabits. In this sense, the ash plant has much in
common with the various other symbolic objects and routines
we have encountered in much of Heaney's later poetry – the
hazel stick and the kite we find in the poems written for his
children, for instance, or the rigidly choreographed routine of
the domestic chores we encounter in 'Clearances', or even the
trawlers of 'Glanmore Sonnets' VII, which prompt Heaney to
forge a connection between the 'marvellous' and the 'actual'.

The complex relationship which is posited in these poems
between the 'marvellous' and the 'actual', or, as we might re-
phrase it, between the transcendent and the material, is entirely
characteristic of the poetic thrust of much of Heaney's later
work. Traditionally, poetry is seen as providing access to a realm
which transcends the immediate world of everyday life. It is
this quality of poetry which Sir Philip Sidney indicates when he
writes in his sixteenth-century *Defence of Poetry* of the capacity
of the writer to deliver a 'golden world', where nature itself
can only deliver a world of brass. In the twentieth century, this
traditional orthodoxy, while sustained in many quarters (notably,
for instance, by W. B. Yeats), has nevertheless increasingly been
subject to interrogation.

Heaney's relationship to the issues of transcendence and materiality is complex. In his earliest poems, we recall, he is profoundly invested in the project of providing a space, within his poems, for the particularities of his immediate, native world. He is inspired in this by his perception of Patrick Kavanagh's poetic project, excited by the prospect of rendering into print what he calls 'the unregarded data of the usual life' (*GT* 7). In such a rendering, the particular comes to assume a more resonant significance, and, in this sense, the transcendent is predicated upon a close engagement with the particular. In Sidney's terms, we might say that the golden world is achieved not by a kind of alchemical transformation of the base metal of the natural world, but rather by focusing on the natural world a poetic eye for detail so acute that it can bring to perception the hitherto unobserved gold within the compound of the everyday.

This sense of the relationship between the material or the particular, on the one hand, and the transcendent, on the other, remains more or less constant throughout Heaney's career. In his later poems, however, we can see Heaney beginning to offer a somewhat more complex sense of the nature of the interface between the material and the transcendent. In his later poems, Heaney, even as he maintains a certain belief in the possibility of transcendence, at the same time maintains a certain sceptical attitude towards that possibility. We can see this balance between faith and scepticism sketched out in a poem such as 'The King of the Ditchbacks' from *Station Island*. The poem is concerned with the process of translation, specifically, with Heaney's own attempts to translate the medieval Irish poem *Buile Suibhne* into English. *Buile Suibhne* is an extremely important work to Heaney (as it has been to a number of other Irish writers – Flann O'Brien incorporated sections of his own translation of the poem into his novel *At Swim-Two-Birds*) and references to the work recur throughout his later poetry.

The poem tells the story of an Irish king, Sweeney, who, following an altercation with the Christian priest, Ronan, is cursed by the priest so that he is transformed into a bird and goes mad. The story has several points of attraction for Heaney. On the one hand, Sweeney serves as a figure for the artist: 'displaced, guilty, assuaging himself by his utterance, it is possible to read the work as an aspect of the quarrel between free creative imagination and the constraints of religious, political, and domestic obligation' (*SA*, Introduction). On the other hand, Heaney's interest in the story is also prompted by the insight it offers into the anxieties prompted by the collision of two cultural systems – native Celtic paganism and the Christian culture which succeeded it. As Heaney himself observes: 'the literary imagination which fastened upon [Sweeney] as an image was clearly in the grip of a tension between the newly dominant Christian ethos and the older, recalcitrant Celtic temperament' (*SA*, Introduction).[5] In this sense, we might see Sweeney as a 'liminal', or threshold, figure, suspended between two worlds – the traditional Celtic world which pledges its faith to an immediate physical realm, and a religious world which offers fidelity to the non-material, the spiritual, the transcendent.

If we turn to 'King of the Ditchbacks' we can see how Sweeney's positioning between these two realms is consonant with Heaney's sense of the relation between the material and the transcendent. In the second section of the poem, Heaney writes of his sense of Sweeney's presence nearby as he was translating the Irish text: 'He was depending on me as I hung out on the limb of a translated phrase like a youngster dared out on to an alder branch over the whirlpool' (*SI* 57). The sentence is deceptive in its clarity and is densely compacted with meaning. Heaney feels himself to be 'out on a limb', taking risks in translating the poem. Sweeney, he tells us, is 'depending' on him. The word 'depending' has a double force here. On the one hand, it indicates the responsibility which the situation imposes on Heaney – Sweeney requires Heaney to translate his story so that his history can be articulated. On the other hand, 'depending' also means 'to hang down, be suspended'. One of the examples of this usage which the *Oxford English Dictionary* offers is Southey's 'The mountain-ash ... depends its branches to the stream below'.[6] So we can see that, in a peculiar way, the text folds in on itself here. Sweeney is reliant on Heaney to tell his story. In this sense, Heaney is forced by his responsibility out onto the branch of creative risk. At the same time, however, Sweeney may also be seen as hanging on Heaney, as the branch Heaney ventures onto itself hangs 'over the whirlpool'. Sweeney is a kind of principle of gravity, pulling Heaney downwards, even as he is also a principle of inspiration, spurring Heaney on to creative effort. Heaney's position, then, is finely – and precariously – balanced between the two forces exerted upon him.

We can see this sense of precarious doubleness at play in the closing section of 'King of the Ditchbacks' also. Here the speaking voice in the poem – which had been the poet's own voice – becomes conflated (or perhaps, more accurately, confused) with a modern Sweeney. The speaker is brought into the woods with his head 'dressed . . . in a fishnet' with 'leafy twigs' plaited through the meshes 'so [his] vision was a bird's | at the heart of a thicket'. After a time, the speaker feels himself experiencing a transformation: 'And I saw myself | rising to move in that dissimulation, | | top-knotted, masked in sheaves, noting | the fall of birds' (*SI* 58). The key word to focus on here is 'dissimulation', which, like 'depending', has a double force in this context. On the one hand, 'dissimulation' means 'the action of . . . dissembling; concealment of what really is, under a feigned semblance of something different; feigning . . . '. So Heaney would appear to be indicating that the transformation experienced by the speaker is really no transformation at all – it is no more than an effect of the speaker's taking on the 'disguise' or 'costume' which is imposed upon him. On the other hand, if we search more closely through the meanings of the word 'dissimulation', we find the following alternative sense of the word: 'A fanciful name for a "company" or flock of small birds'.[7] Adopting this meaning of the word, the lines in question take on a quite different sense, since, in this instance, the lines indicate a literal and actual transformation – the speaker, having become a bird himself, sees himself rise to move as part of a company of birds.

This sense of doubleness, of affirming a certain faith in transcendence while at the same time retaining a sense of that transcendence as possibly being no more than a delusion – or, alternatively, of affirming faith in transcendence in defiance of the knowledge that transcendence is, objectively, no more than a delusion – is central to Heaney's most recent poetry, particularly in his 1991 volume *Seeing Things*. The very title of this collection rests precisely upon this sense of doubleness, in that it simultaneously indicates poetry's power to *per*ceive and to *de*ceive. 'Field of Vision' is a good example of the way in which

Heaney pursues this theme in *Seeing Things*. Again, the title of the poem has a double inflection. The poem is about a woman who sits in a wheelchair, staring fixedly out into the countryside. Heaney compares her sight to the sight one experiences looking beyond 'a well-braced gate' into a field. The 'field of vision' of the title can be either the full extent of what one sees, or it can be the particular literal field, bounded by hedges, that lies beyond the gate which bars the viewer's way. Or, again, 'vision' itself can have a deeper, more mystical sense – it can be a felt perception which is either real or imaginary, as, for instance, in the case of a religious vision. Standing at the gate, we are told, you could see

> Deeper into the country than you expected
> And discovered that the field behind the hedge
> Grew more distinctly strange as you kept standing
> Focused and drawn in by what barred the way.
>
> (*ST* 22)

Here, again, as in the case of poems such as 'The Ash Plant', 'I.I.87', or 'A Hazel Stick for Catherine Ann', it is a solid material object which facilitates a peculiar kind of 'access' to the immaterial. The barrier of the gate is, ironically, what enables the viewer to penetrate more clearly the strangeness of the space which lies beyond it. In this sense, the poet imagines for the viewer an experience not unlike that of looking at a perceptual illusion such as the three-dimensional illustration of a cube which, if stared at fixedly, oscillates between appearing to come out of the page in one of two opposing directions. What we see in our field of vision is, likewise, Heaney seems to be suggesting, a flickering between the material and the visionary.

What interests Heaney here is precisely the threshold experience – the experience of being situated between two different states or conditions. This is, of course, we will recall, one of the features of the Sweeney story which Heaney found attractive. We can trace Heaney's own biographical sense of liminality in a poem such as 'Terminus' from *The Haw Lantern*. 'I grew up in between' (*HL* 5), he writes, and, in marked contrast to the unambiguously rural milieu of *Death of a Naturalist*, he indicates how the modern industrial world cast its shadow over his country childhood:

When I hoked there, I would find
An acorn and a rusted bolt.

If I lifted my eyes, a factory chimney
And a dormant mountain.

If I listened, an engine shunting
And a trotting horse.

(*HL* 4)

The notion of the liminal, of negotiating between one realm or state and another, is central to the vision of *Seeing Things*, as Heaney exhorts himself to 'Relocate the bedrock in the threshold' (*ST* 56). An entire section of the second half of the book is given over to a group of poems with the general title 'Crossings', in the opening piece of which Heaney finds himself 'in the middle of the road' (*ST* 83) – echoing the opening line of Dante's *Divine Comedy*, which Heaney directly quotes earlier in the volume (in 'The Schoolbag'): '*nel mezzo del cammin*' ('in the middle of the way'). Likewise, Heaney closes *Seeing Things* with a piece entitled 'The Crossing'. This poem is, in fact, a translation of a section of Canto III of the *Inferno*, which details the poet's encountering of Charon – the mythical boatman who carries the souls of the dead over the River Styx to the underworld. This translation balances exactly another translation set at the opening of the volume – a section of Virgil's *Aeneid*, in which Aeneas seeks to venture into the underworld to encounter his dead father.

In the *Inferno*, it is the poet, Dante himself, accompanied by another poet, Virgil, who can make the journey which no other mortal can survive. Only Dante can return from the other world of the dead to the living world of everyday life. In the *Aeneid*, the hero can only make his journey and return if he carries with him a symbolic object – 'a bough made of gold | And its leaves and pliable twigs are made of it too' (*ST* 3). In a sense, we might say, returning (anachronistically) to Sidney, that Aeneas' double journey is only possible if it is facilitated by a token derived from the 'golden world' of artifice; likewise the journey of Dante to and from the underworld is a journey which only he, as a poet, can make. Viewed in this light, the essential thrust of *Seeing Things* is to suggest that the function of poetry (or of art generally) is precisely to sustain the threshold between different realms – to hold open the possibility of a negotiation between such realms. As Heaney observes in *The Government of the Tongue*: 'Poetry is more a threshold than a path, one constantly approached and constantly departed from, at which the reader and writer undergo in their different ways the experience of being at the same time summoned and released' (*GT* 108). The fundamental point of poetry is not to effect an arrival but to facilitate the possibility of 'crossings' – a fruitful interrelation of, we might say, the worlds of possibility and materiality.

This sense of the possibility of maintaining a fruitful channel between the mundane and the marvellous is finely caught by Heaney in one of the most striking poems included in *Seeing Things* – viii in the 'Lightenings' section of the volume. The poem offers us a fanciful anecdote from the Irish historical annals. As the monks at the abbey of Clonmacnoise are at prayer, a ship appears in the air above them. The ship is dragging its anchor, which becomes caught in the chapel's altar rail. A member of the crew of the ship climbs down the rope and tries unsuccessfully to release it. The abbot suggests that the monks must intervene to save the man's life:

'This man can't bear our life here and will drown,'
The abbot said, 'unless we help him.' So
They did, the freed ship sailed, and the man climbed back
Out of the marvellous as he had known it.

(*ST* 62)

What the poem suggests is that the marvellous and the actual are not divorced, antithetical realms, but rather that there is a consonance between the two. As Henry Hart has noted, like the American poet Marianne Moore, Heaney realizes that 'the visionary and the real are symbiotic rather than exclusive'.[8] The quotidian world of the monks constitutes the marvellous for the sailor of the visionary ship, just as his world in turn, constitutes the marvellous for the monks themselves. What the poet offers, in Heaney's view, is a channel of negotiation between these two territories.

In noting the connection between the views of poetry put forward by Heaney and by Marianne Moore, Henry Hart reminds us of Moore's famously calling for a poetry which offers 'imaginary gardens with real toads in them'. Heaney's first published book concerns itself very much with 'real toads', with the particulars of his rural surroundings, the flora and fauna of country life. In pursuing a poetic of this kind, Heaney was, we have noted, being faithful to the values which he perceived in the poetry of Patrick Kavanagh – a poetry which celebrated 'the unregarded data of the usual life'. Heaney writes in *The Government of the Tongue* that in the 1960s he 'was still more susceptible to the pathos and familiarity of the matter of Kavanagh's poetry than . . . alert to the liberation and subversiveness of its manner' (*GT* 10). Later in life, Heaney developed a more complex sense of what Kavanagh was seeking to achieve in his work. He began to perceive a shift in Kavanagh's poetic practice between the first and second halves of his career. The early Kavanagh, Heaney proposes, 'is pervious to this world's spirit more than it is pervious to his spirit . . . the experienced physical reality of Monaghan life imposes itself upon the poet's consciousness so that he necessarily composes himself, his poetic identity and his poems in relation to that encircling horizon of given experience'. (*GT* 5) By contrast, he suggests, 'a definite change is perceptible' in Kavanagh's later poetry:

> We might say that now the world is more pervious to his vision than he is pervious to the world. When he writes about places now, they are luminous spaces within his mind. They have been evacuated of their status as background, as documentary geography, and exist instead as transfigured images, sites where the mind projects its own force. In this later poetry, place is included within the horizon of Kavanagh's mind rather than the other way around.

In writing about Kavanagh here Heaney is also, in a way, writing about himself. The early Heaney too is 'pervious to the world', seeking to be faithful to its particulars. In the later Heaney, as in the later Kavanagh (or, at least, in Heaney's perception of the later Kavanagh), world becomes pervious to mind, as the particular becomes less important than the realm to which it gives access – the territory upon which mind can play. But perhaps, finally, for Heaney what is important is not so much mind or world in and of itself, but rather the state of perviousness that brings them into interaction. What interests Heaney in the end is no longer either the real toads or the imaginary gardens, but rather the process of bringing the two together and the interaction to which that conjunction gives rise.

Postscript

Throughout this volume we have focused our attention primarily on Seamus Heaney's position as an Irish poet, deeply indebted to a poetic tradition which ranges from the *dinnseanchas* conventions of the bardic schools of Gaelic poetry to influential twentieth-century poets such as Patrick Kavanagh and W. B. Yeats. In addition, we have seen Heaney's poetry as being concerned first and foremost with native political, historical, and cultural themes. It should be noted, however, that Heaney's work is also indebted to poetic models and modes of thinking which are not native to Ireland and that, the firm grounding of his poetry in Irish soil notwithstanding, Heaney's work has an appeal which extends far beyond his native country.

One striking aspect of Heaney's poetry in this regard is the extent to which Heaney is, like Yeats before him, so drawn to the literature of the English Renaissance. Again and again we find him returning to the work of his sixteenth- and seventeenth-century English predecessors – Thomas Wyatt, Edmund Spenser, Walter Ralegh, William Shakespeare. While Heaney sometimes offers a critical engagement with these writers – with both Spenser and Ralegh appearing in his poetry as emblematic figures of English imperialism – he also accepts the literary inheritance which these writers offer, drawing on their work itself and on the forms and poetic conventions which they helped to establish. Throughout his career, Heaney has also been indebted to more recent English writers – for instance, Gerard Manley Hopkins and Ted Hughes (in *Death of a Naturalist* and elsewhere in the early poetry) and Thomas Hardy (especially in *Seeing Things*).

This English dimension of his work perhaps helps in some measure to explain the degree of success which Heaney has enjoyed in Britain. His major works have always been published by the London-based firm of Faber and Faber and his books have sold widely in Britain. It is a marker of this success that, in December 1995, Heaney's *New Selected Poems* was included in a book-club advertisement in a UK Sunday newspaper – standing shoulder to shoulder with novels by Stephen King and Anne Rice.[1] But Heaney's success in Britain has extended beyond the purely commercial. Throughout his writing career, he has received numerous British literary awards, including the Somerset Maugham Award in 1967, the W. H. Smith Award in 1975, and the Whitbread Award in 1987. Commercial and critical success have also been accompanied by academic success; in 1988 Heaney was elected to the professorship of poetry at Oxford University. The poet has sometimes been troubled by the implications of this British success, and he has registered this anxiety most notably (and humorously) in his *Open Letter* to Blake Morrison and Andrew Motion, objecting to his work being included in a collection of contemporary *British* poetry. In a more serious vein, in *The Redress of Poetry*, Heaney has written about his profound discomfort at being the recipient of the hospitality of the British high cultural establishment at Oxford, on the night when a near neighbour from the north of Ireland died on hunger strike, as part of a protest seeking the reinstatement of political status for IRA prisoners.

'[B]e advised I My passport's green. I No glass of ours was ever raised I To toast *The Queen*',[2] Heaney writes in *An Open Letter*, but there always seems to have been a fundamental ambivalence in his attitude to England and to its culture. Be that as it may, Heaney's Irish passport has also taken him to places far beyond Britain and Ireland during the course of his career as a poet. In 1970–1, Heaney spent a year teaching as a guest lecturer at the Berkeley campus of the University of California. The Belfast he left in 1970 was in a state of deepening crisis. The British Army had been deployed on the streets in the previous year and, while Heaney was away, the government introduced a policy of 'internment' – imprisoning more than 1,500 people without benefit of trial. His stay in the USA left Heaney feeling dispirited when he returned to Belfast – he described the return to Northern Ireland as 'like putting on an old dirty glove again'. The USA, he observed, 'gave me the idea that I would have to come back and say that this place is a kind of disease preventing personality from flowering gracefully. It is a very graceless community, a very scared and stunted community.'[3]

Heaney has maintained his US connections over the course of the past decades. In 1979 he spent a term at Harvard University in Boston, as a temporary successor to the American poet Robert Lowell. In 1982 he was back at Harvard, having accepted a five-year contract to teach at the university for one semester each year. Two years later he was elected to Harvard's prestigious Boylston Chair of Rhetoric and Oratory. Despite the strength of Heaney's US connections, the impact of his American experience on his poetry is oddly hard to trace. Certainly, he has been influenced by the work of a number of contemporary American poets, and Robert Lowell is very much a case in point. Heaney became a close personal friend of Lowell while living in Boston and he has observed that he 'loved the ignorance' of Lowell's poetry; 'the bull-headedness, the rage and the uncharmingness of the writing attracted me enormously.' As Michael Parker has observed, Heaney's conception of Lowell's project has much in common with his own expressed ambition that in *North* he wished 'to take the English lyric and make it eat stuff that it has never eaten before'.[4] In *Field Work*'s 'Elegy' Heaney acknowledges his debt to Lowell, calling him 'the master elegist | and welder of English' (*FW* 31). Likewise, in his prose writings, Heaney has acknowledged the importance to his writing of other American poets, such as Theodore Roethke and Sylvia Plath.

America itself is featured here and there in Heaney's poems. It appears tangentially in 'Bogland', which takes as its point of departure the notion of 'the frontier and the west as an important myth in the American consciousness' (*P*. 55). *Wintering Out*'s 'Westering' is set, as the subtitle tells us, '*In California*', and, occasionally (as in the case of 'The Skunk' and *Station Island*'s 'Remembering Malibu') we find a poem that is firmly located in an American landscape. It is striking, however, that – for a poet who spends a significant part of every year in Boston – American culture, concerns, geography, and idiom feature so little in Heaney's work. One might contrast him in this regard with his fellow Irish poet Brian Coffey, who distils and meditates upon his American experience in an extended set of poems, entitled *Missouri Sequence*, or with contemporary Irish novelists such as Joseph O'Connor and Colm Tobín, whose experiences living in

Nicaragua and Spain respectively have been reflected in their writing.

Some might argue that Heaney's resistance to American culture and subject matter in some sense indicates a certain insular parochialism in his work. But it is also possible to argue that recent years have witnessed a considerable broadening of Heaney's poetic scope. It is indicative of this broader focus that Heaney has found himself drawing his inspiration from eastern European poets, notably Zbigniew Herbert, Czeslaw Milosz, and Miroslav Holub. The effect on Heaney's poetry of this work has been to render it less specific, more abstract. The particularities of native landscapes are set aside, as in poems such as 'From the Canton of Expectation', 'Parable Island', and 'From the Republic of Conscience' Heaney presents us with a generalized, abstract location. In so far as these poems are situated in Ireland at all, it is a highly metaphorized and mythologized Ireland, as 'From the Republic of Conscience' indicates:

> The woman in customs asked me to declare
> the words of our traditional cures and charms
> to heal dumbness and avert the evil eye.
>
> No porters. No interpreter. No taxi.
> You carried your own burden and very soon
> your symptoms of creeping privilege disappeared.
>
> (*HL* 12)

With this broadening of Heaney's canvas has come a broadening of his appeal as a poet, so that, having long been established in Ireland, Britain, and the USA, in recent years he has increasingly come to be viewed as a poet of truly international standing. It is indicative of this widening of his reputation that Heaney was, in 1995, awarded the Nobel Prize for Literature, with the Nobel committee commending him, in their citation, for his 'works of lyrical beauty and ethical depth, which exalt everyday miracles and the living past'.[5]

It seems entirely appropriate that the previous Irish writer known primarily for his poetry to have received the Nobel Prize was W. B. Yeats. As noted in the Introduction to this volume, Heaney and Yeats share a complex sense of the poet's responsibility in and to his or her own particular political and cultural moment. Heaney has been one of a relatively small group of contemporary writers willing, like Yeats, to bring a sense of true commitment and complexity to the role of the poet. As the Irish President, Mary Robinson, observed in her message to the poet, congratulating him on having received the Nobel Prize, Heaney's work has 'excited, enlightened, challenged and inspired, but never disappointed'.[6]

Appendix

Some part of the island of Ireland has been under the dominion of Britain since the late twelfth century. Broadly speaking, the relationship between the two islands has always been colonial in nature, and at least some element of the Irish population has always been hostile to the domination of the island by the British. Early in the seventeenth century, at a time when native Irish power had been decisively broken following a war which had lasted for nine years, one of the largest colonising projects ever was undertaken in Ireland. A large group of mainly Scots Presbyterian settlers (the native Irish were, by contrast, mostly Roman Catholic) were introduced into the northern part of Ireland as part of this colonizing scheme. Native Irish resistance to colonization and to British rule continued over the centuries that followed.

By the early decades of the twentieth century, it became clear that some form of British disengagement from the island would be necessary. The difficulty was that, even as the native Irish section of the population wished to break the link, or 'union', with Britain, the descendents of the colonial community wanted to retain that link (thus becoming characterized as 'unionists', or 'loyalists'). As a compromise to the complex demands of the island's different communities – and partly in response to a militant nationalist uprising in 1916 – the British partitioned the island. In 1921 the six northernmost counties (which included the greatest concentration of 'unionists', mostly Protestant in religion) were granted their own parliament, as a semi-autonomous region within the UK. In the following year, the insurrectionary forces fighting to break the link with Britain agreed by a narrow margin to accept the terms of a treaty offered to them by the British (including the partition of the island), and, as a result, the remaining twenty-six counties of the island were granted the status of a 'Free State'. In 1948, the parliament of the Free State voted to declare the twenty-six counties a republic, thus severing the country's remaining governmental ties with Britain.

Partition tended to polarize the island politically and religiously. The south was overwhelmingly Roman Catholic, and, with no adequate attempt being made to separate Church and State, a Catholic ethos dominated the Constitution (approved by parliament in 1937), the educational system, and public life in general. In Northern Ireland, by contrast, about 60 per cent of the population was Protestant. This Protestant majority, fearing encroachment from the Catholic-dominated south, set about systematically concentrating power in its own hands. Catholics were discriminated against in housing, employment, and education, and by a process of gerrymandering (the massaging of constituency boundaries, and so on), Catholics were deprived of power even in those areas where they were in the majority. In the late 1960s, following the example of the Civil Rights movement in the USA, a series of protests were held to seek an end to discriminatory practices in the North. These protests were rigorously opposed by the Northern Irish authorities. As the situation deteriorated, militant nationalist anti-unionists (principally the Irish Republican Army (IRA)) and militant pro-unionists increasingly took a hand in the conflict. The introduction of the British Army onto the streets of the North served to focus nationalist grievances still further (the British were seen by nationalists as a pro-unionist occupying force), as did a series of punitive measures imposed from London by the government at Westminster. From 1970 onwards the province drifted into a period of bloodshed, with frequent bombings, shootings, and sectarian murders. Various attempts to solve the crisis have so far failed.

Notes

INTRODUCTION

1. Patrick Kavanagh, *Collected Poems* (London, 1972), p. xiii.
2. For those less well versed in the details of the conflict in Northern Ireland, I have included a very short survey of the history of the conflict as an appendix to this volume. Please note that this appendix is not intended to be anything other than a very broadly sketched and condensed overview; readers who require a more detailed account should consult some of the works listed in the Further Reading Section of the Select Bibliography.
3. W. B. Yeats, *Collected Poems* (London, 1982), 243.
4. In weighing the responsibilities of the poet, Heaney aligns himself with the Russian poet Osip Mandelstam as much as with Yeats. See *GT* 71–90.
5. Yeats, *Collected Poems*, 151. See also the next poem in the collection: 'An Irish Airman Foresees His Death'.

CHAPTER 1. 'LIVING ROOTS AWAKEN IN MY HEAD': PLACE AND DISPLACEMENT

1. Neil Corcoran, *A Student's Guide to Seamus Heaney* (London, 1986), 44.
2. Andrew Waterman, 'The best way out is always through', in Elmer Andrews (ed.), *Seamus Heaney: A Collection of Critical Essays* (London, 1992), 12.
3. Heaney's gesture here is not unlike that of Yeats when, addressing his ancestors in his preface to *Responsibilities*, he writes: 'Although I have come close on forty-nine, | I have no child, I have nothing but a book, | Nothing but that to prove your blood and mine' (*Collected Poems* (London, 1982), 113).
4. In his poems on childhood and familial conflict Heaney is greatly influenced by the US poet Theodore Roethke. See, in particular, Roethke's *The Lost Son and Other Poems*, included in *The Collected Poems of Theodore Roethke* (London, 1966).

5. Michael Parker, *Seamus Heaney: The Making of the Poet* (London, 1993), 66.
6. Patricia Coughlan, ' "Bog Queens": The Representation of Women in the Poetry of John Montague and Seamus Heaney', in Toni O'Brien Johnson and David Cairns (eds.), *Gender in Irish Writing* (Milton Keynes, 1991), 99.
7. Patrick Kavanagh, *Collected Poems* (London, 1972), 136.
8. Seamus Heaney, 'Kavanagh of the Parish', *Listener*, 26 Apr. 1979, p. 577.
9. Homer, *The Iliad*, trans. Robert Fitzgerald (New York, 1975), bk. 18, ll. 554–9.
10. Philip Sidney, *A Defence of Poetry* (Oxford, 1966), 24. See Robert Welch, ' "A rich young man leaving everything he had": Poetic Freedom in Seamus Heaney', in Andrews (ed.), *Seamus Heaney*, 151–2.
11. Place-names have a particular kind of political history in Ireland, indicative of the island's colonial past. Some native Irish place-names survive in their original form, but many others – like 'Anahorish' – were anglicized by the colonists, thus erasing their original meaning value. In other cases, the Irish name has been completely lost, having been replaced by an unrelated new English name. For an interesting dramatization of such issues of naming, see Brian Friel's play *Translations*.
12. Corcoran, *Student's Guide*, 90.
13. I am presuming that 'riverback', in the 1993 edition of *Wintering Out*, is a typographical error. *New Selected Poems* gives what I take to be the correct 'riverbank' (p. 25).

CHAPTER 2. 'WHERE THE FAULT IS OPENING': POLITICS AND MYTHOLOGY

1. Interview with Seamus Deane, 'Unhappy and at Home', *Crane Bag*, 1/1 (1977), 5.
2. Michael Parker, *Seamus Heaney: The Making of the Poet* (London, 1993), 95.
3. Edmund Spenser, *A View of the Present State of Ireland*, in R. Morris (ed.), *The Complete Works of Edmund Spenser* (London, 1869), 654.
4. Karl Marx, *The Eighteenth Brumaire of Louis Bonaparte*, in Robert C. Tucker (ed.), *The Marx–Engels Reader* (New York, 1978), 594.
5. Parker, *Seamus Heaney*, 106.
6. Quoted in Neil Corcoran, *A Student's Guide to Seamus Heaney* (London, 1986), 96
7. Ibid. 78.
8. Bernard O'Donoghue, *Seamus Heaney and the Language of Poetry* (Hemel Hempstead, 1994), 6.

9. Heaney in an interview with Harriet Cooke, quoted in Corcoran, *Student's Guide*, 95.

10. See Parker, *Seamus Heaney*, 131. Parker draws on Heaney's commentary for a 1980 BBC film entitled *The Boyne Valley*, directed by David Hammond.

11. R. F. Foster, *Modern Ireland, 1600–1972* (London, 1989), 142.

12. Blake Morrison, *Seamus Heaney* (London, 1982), 68.

CHAPTER 3. 'I HEAR AGAIN THE SURE CONFUSING DRUM': REVERSIONS AND REVISIONS

1. James Simmons, 'The Trouble with Seamus', in Elmer Andrews (ed.), *Seamus Heaney: A Collection of Critical Essays*, 59.

2. Edna Longley, *Poetry in the Wars* (Newcastle, 1986), 185. Longley has refined this observation in her more recent *The Living Stream: Literature and Revisionism in Ireland* (Newcastle, 1994), in which she observes: 'by politics I meant predatory ideologies, fixed agendas and fixed expectations' (p. 9).

3. Desmond Fennell, *Whatever You Say, Say Nothing* (Dublin, 1991), 16–17.

4. Ciarán Carson, 'Escaped from the Massacre?', *Honest Ulsterman*, 50 (Winter 1975).

5. David Lloyd, *Anomalous States: Irish Writing and the Post-Colonial Moment* (Dublin, 1993), 27. Lloyd's chapter on Heaney in *Anomalous States* is also included in Andrews (ed.), *Seamus Heaney*.

6. Heaney's sense of mythology and of the relationship between myth and history is also rather more complex than writers such as Carson and Lloyd allow. Heaney's views are in part informed by Richard Kearney's *Myth and Motherland* (included in *Ireland's Field Day* (Notre Dame, Ind., 1986)), which sets out a sophisticated reading of the relationship between history and mythology.

7. Seamus Deane, 'Talk with Seamus Heaney', *New York Times Review*, 84/48 (1979), 48.

8. Maurice Harmon, '"We Pine for Ceremony": Ritual and Reality in the Poetry of Seamus Heaney, 1965–75', in Andrews (ed.), *Seamus Heaney*, 76.

9. See Michael Parker, *Seamus Heaney: The Making of the Poet* (London, 1993), 162.

10. Dante, *The Divine Comedy 2: Purgatorio*, trans. John D. Sinclair (Oxford, 1961), 25.

11. Neil Corcoran, *A Student's Guide to Seamus Heaney* (London, 1986), 163.

12. In *The Redress of Poetry*, Heaney writes of his sense of having in some way 'betrayed' his community as he enjoyed the hospitality of the British establishment at Oxford on the night that Hughes died.

CHAPTER 4. 'IT WAS MARVELLOUS AND ACTUAL': FAMILIARITY AND FANTASY

1. Quoted in Neil Corcoran, *A Student's Guide to Seamus Heaney* (London, 1986), 128.
2. *Collected Poems of Sir Thomas Wyatt*, ed. Kenneth Muir (Cambridge, Mass., 1950), 28.
3. *Selected Poems and Prefaces by William Wordsworth*, ed. Jack Stillinger (Boston, 1965), 108.
4. Blake Morrison, *And When Did You Last See Your Father?* (London, 1994), 191, 198.
5. Yeats also writes about this clash of cultures, in taking up the traditional story of an imagined encounter between the dying mythical Celtic hero Oisín and St Patrick, who is said to have brought the Christian faith to Ireland. See his 'Wanderings of Oisin'.
6. *The Compact Edition of the Oxford English Dictionary* (Oxford, 1971), 689.
7. Ibid. 765.
8. Henry Hart, 'What is Heaney Seeing in *Seeing Things?*', *Colby Quarterly*, 30/1 (Mar. 1994), 33.

POSTSCRIPT

1. See *Observer Life*, 3 Dec. 1995, pp. 56–7.
2. Seamus Heaney, 'An Open Letter', in *Ireland's Field Day* (Notre Dame, Ind., 1986), 25.
3. Quoted in Michael Parker, *Seamus Heaney: The Making of the Poet* (London, 1993), 117.
4. Quoted in ibid. 122, 123.
5. Quoted in *Guardian*, 6 Oct. 1995, p. 1.
6. Ibid.

Select Bibliography

WORKS BY SEAMUS HEANEY

Death of a Naturalist (London: Faber & Faber, 1966).
A Lough Neagh Sequence (Manchester: Phoenix Pamphlet Poets, 1966).
Door into the Dark (London: Faber & Faber, 1969).
Wintering Out (London: Faber & Faber, 1972).
Soundings (Belfast: Blackstaff, 1972).
Stations (Belfast: Ulsterman, 1975).
Bog Poems (London: Rainbow, 1975).
North (London: Faber & Faber, 1975).
Field Work (London: Faber & Faber, 1979).
Preoccupations: Selected Prose 1968–1978 (London: Faber & Faber, 1980).
Selected Poems 1965–1975 (London: Faber & Faber, 1980).
The Rattle Bag: An Anthology of Poetry, as editor, with Ted Hughes (London: Faber & Faber, 1982).
An Open Letter (Derry: Field Day, 1983; repr. in *Ireland's Field Day*, Notre Dame, Ind. 1986).
Sweeney Astray (Derry: Field Day, 1983; London: Faber & Faber, 1984).
Station Island (London: Faber & Faber, 1984).
Hailstones (Dublin: Gallery, 1985).
Clearances (Dublin: Cornamona, 1986).
The Haw Lantern (London: Faber & Faber, 1987).
The Government of the Tongue: The 1986 T. S. Eliot Memorial Lectures and Other Critical Writings (London: Faber & Faber, 1988).
The Cure at Troy: A Version of Sophocles' Philoctetes (London: Faber & Faber, 1990).
The Tree-Clock (Belfast: Linen Hall Library, 1990).
New Selected Poems 1966–1987 (London: Faber & Faber, 1990).
Seeing Things (London: Faber & Faber, 1991).
The Redress of Poetry (London: Faber & Faber, 1995).

INTERVIEWS

In excess of twenty-five interviews with the poet have been published. Major interviews include:

Brandes, Rand, *Salmagundi*, 80 (Fall 1988).
Cooke, Harriet, *Irish Times*, 28 Dec. 1973.
Deane, Seamus, 'Unhappy and at Home', *Crane Bag*, 1/1 (1977).
— 'Talk', *New York Times Book Review*, 2 Dec. 1979.
Druce, Robert, 'A Raindrop on a Thorn', *Dutch Quarterly Review*, 9 (1978).
Haffenden, John, 'Meeting Seamus Heaney', *London Magazine* (June 1979).
Kinahan, Frank, *Critical Inquiry*, 8/3 (Spring 1982).
Randall, James, 'An Interview with Seamus Heaney', *Ploughshares*, 5/3 (1979).

CRITICAL STUDIES

Rand Brandes and Michael J. Durkan, *Seamus Heaney: A Reference Guide* (New York, 1994), provides a comprehensive guide to available materials on Heaney. For a shorter survey of Heaney scholarship, see Brandes's extremely useful brief history of Heaney reception, 'Secondary Sources: A Gloss on the Critical Reception of Seamus Heaney 1965–1993', in the *Colby Quarterly* issue listed below.

Books

Andrews, Elmer, *The Poetry of Seamus Heaney: All in the Realms of Whisper* (London, 1989). A useful, clear introduction to Heaney's poetry.
— (ed.), *Seamus Heaney: A Collection of Critical Essays* (London, 1992). Andrews's 'Introduction' is particularly useful and the volume includes interesting pieces by John Lucas and Terence Brown. James Simmons's 'The Trouble with Seamus' provides a rather lightweight critique of the poet, but is worth reading. The volume also reprints David Lloyd's 'Pap for the Dispossessed' – probably the best negative assessment of Heaney's work currently in print.
Bloom, Harold (ed.), *Seamus Heaney* (New York, 1986). A good general collection of articles on Heaney.
Byron, Catherine, *Out of Step: Pursuing Seamus Heaney to Purgatory* (Loxwood, UK, 1992). Particularly strong in offering a broadly sympathetic feminist reading of *Station Island*.
Corcoran, Neil, *A Student's Guide to Seamus Heaney* (London, 1986). The title does something of an injustice to this book, as Corcoran provides more than just an introductory guide. His book is clear, sophisticated,

and engaging, though, having been published in 1986, it does not cover Heaney's recent writing.

Curtis, Tony (ed.), *The Art of Seamus Heaney* (3rd edn., Bridgend, Wales, 1994). This collection has been updated several times and contains a number of useful pieces on Heaney's poetry.

Hart, Henry, *Seamus Heaney: Poet of Contrary Progressions* (New York, 1992). Probably the most sophisticated, theoretically oriented book on Heaney currently available.

Morrison, Blake, *Seamus Heaney* (London, 1982). The first book-length study of Heaney's work. Morrison's short book is now very much outdated, but still provides an interesting introduction to Heaney's early work.

O'Donoghue, Bernard, *Seamus Heaney and the Language of Poetry* (Hemel Hempstead, 1994). As the title suggests, O'Donoghue's book focuses almost exclusively on the language of the poems. Indispensable for anyone interested in the linguistic aspect of Heaney's work.

Parker, Michael, *Seamus Heaney: The Making of the Poet* (London, 1993). Parker provides interesting commentary on Heaney's work, but the real subject of his book is the poet's life. The book provides a wealth of information on Heaney's background and the context in which his poems were produced. A standard reference work for anyone writing on Heaney.

Tamplin, Ronald, *Seamus Heaney* (Milton Keynes, 1989). Produced as part of the Open University 'Open Guides' series, this is a rather disappointing book which, while useful in providing a general introduction to the poet's work, is rather limited in the insights which it offers.

Articles

An enormous number of articles on Heaney have been published over the years. The following offers no more than a flavour of some useful recent criticism.

Allison, Jonathan, 'Acts of Union: Seamus Heaney's Tropes of Sex and Marriage', *Éire-Ireland*, 27/4 (1992). An interesting commentary on Heaney's marriage imagery, set usefully within the context of notions of political union.

Carson, Ciarán, 'Escaped from the Massacre?', *Honest Ulsterman*, 50 (Winter 1975). A telling and astute review of *North* by a fellow Northern Irish poet, who takes Heaney to task for political imprecision.

Colby Quarterly, 30/1 (Mar. 1994). This is a special issue of *Colby Quarterly* dedicated to Heaney's work. It contains Rand Brandes's review of Heaney reception from 1965 to 1993, as well as very interesting articles by Henry Hart (on *Seeing Things*) and Elizabeth Butler Cullingford.

Coughlan, Patricia, ' "Bog Queens": The Representation of Women in the Poetry of John Montague and Seamus Heaney', in Toni O'Brien Johnson and David Cairns (eds.), *Gender in Irish Writing* (Milton Keynes, 1991). An interesting feminist critique of Heaney's use of gendered imagery and metaphors.

Cullingford, Elizabeth Butler, 'Thinking of Her . . . as . . . Ireland: Yeats, Pearse, and Heaney', *Textual Practice*, 4/1 (Spring 1990). A useful commentary on the intersection between nationalism and gender.

Deane, Seamus, 'Seamus Heaney: The Timorous and the Bold', in *Celtic Revivals* (London, 1985). An assessment of Heaney's work by his friend and fellow Field Day director.

Fennell, Desmond, *Whatever You Say, Say Nothing* (Dublin, 1991). A pamphlet attacking Heaney as a poet who has courted popularity with international audiences without offering anything of real substance in his poetry. The piece is rather lightweight and is belligerent in a crudely personal way, but nevertheless does offer some cogent criticism of Heaney's work and what might be called 'the Heaney phenomenon'.

Longley, Edna, 'Poetry and Politics in Northern Ireland', in *Poetry in the Wars* (Newcastle, UK, 1986). Part of this chapter is devoted to an examination of the politics of Heaney's poetry, especially as expressed in *North*. Longley, who might broadly be said not to be sympathetic to the nationalist political agenda, offers a useful and interesting critique of Heaney's political stance.

Smith, Stan, 'The Distance Between', in Neil Corcoran (ed.), *The Chosen Ground: Essays on Contemporary Poetry in Northern Ireland* (Bridgend, Wales, 1992). A cogent, theoretically informed assessment of Heaney's recent poetry.

Wills, Clair, 'Language Politics, Narrative, Political Violence', *Oxford Literary Review*, 13/1–2 (1991). A sophisticated article on the politics of Heaney's language, with includes a useful interrogation of Heaney's use of gender.

FURTHER READING

The literary context

Brown, Terence, *Northern Voices: Poets from Ulster* (Dublin, 1975).

— *Ireland's Literature: Selected Essays* (Mullingar, Ireland, 1989).

Deane, Seamus, *Celtic Revivals* (London, 1985).

— *A Short History of Irish Literature* (London, 1986).

Longley, Edna, *Poetry in the Wars* (Newcastle, 1986).

— *The Living Stream: Literature and Revisionism in Ireland* (Newcastle, 1994).

Lloyd, David, *Anomalous States: Irish Writing and the Post-Colonial Moment* (Dublin, 1993).

The historical and political context

Cairns, David, and Shaun Richards, *Writing Ireland: Colonialism, Nationalism and Culture* (Manchester, 1988). A survey of English writing on the subject of Ireland.

Coogan, Tim Pat, *The IRA* (rev. edn., London, 1987). A standard account of the militant Irish nationalist movement.

— *The Troubles: Ireland's Ordeal 1966–1995 and the Search for Peace* (London, 1995). An account of the most recent decades of the Anglo-Irish conflict.

Curtis, Liz, *Nothing but the Same Old Story: The Roots of Anti-Irish Racism* (London, 1985). A short history of English attitudes towards the Irish.

Devlin, Bernadette, *The Price of my Soul* (London, 1969). An autobiographical account of the early days of the Northern Irish Civil Rights movement by a Derry activist who served for a time as Member of Parliament for Derry.

Farrell, Michael, *Northern Ireland: The Orange State* (London, 1980). A comprehensive history of the Northern Irish state, told from a socialist, nationalist perspective.

Foster, R. F., *Modern Ireland: 1600–1972* (London, 1989). A good, single-volume history of Ireland from the seventeenth to the twentieth centuries.

— *Paddy and Mr. Punch: Connections in Irish and English History* (London, 1993). A collection of essays on culture and history in an Anglo-Irish context.

Ireland's Field Day (Notre Dame, Ind., 1986). A selection of the first group of pamphlets on Irish political and cultural topics published by the Field Day Company, of which Heaney is a director. Includes Heaney's 'An Open Letter'.

McCann, Eamonn, *War and an Irish Town* (rev. edn., London, 1993). A personal account of life in Derry during the Civil Rights era, by a fellow ex-pupil of Heaney's secondary school.

Index

Alighieri, Dante
  Divine Comedy, 59, 61, 71–2, 84
Armstrong, Sean, 58, 64–5

Buile Suibhne, 80–2

Carleton, William, 63–4
  The Lough Derg Pilgrim, 63
Carson, Ciarán, 49–50, 53, 66, 67
Coffey, Brian
  Missouri Sequence, 89
Corcoran, Neil, 10, 26, 62
Coughlan, Patricia, 17

Deane, Seamus, 51
Devlin, Marie, 17
Dinnseanchas (placename poetry), 23, 27, 33, 87
Donnelley, Brian, 37

Ewart-Biggs, Christopher, 55

Fennell, Desmond, 51, 66
  Whatever You Say, Say Nothing, 48–9
Foster, Roy, 41
Friel, Brian, 67, 69

Glob, P. V.
  The Bog People, 33, 36–7, 41, 42–3
Gospel According to St. John, 43

Hammond, David, 1–3, 6, 28
Hardy, Thomas, 87
Harmon, Maurice, 53–4
Hart, Henry, 85
Heaney, Seamus
  'I.I.87', 78–9, 83
  'Act of Union', 45–6

'An Advancement of Learning', 15–16
'After a Killing', 55–6
'An Afterwards', 71
'Anahorish', 23–5
'The Ash Plant', 78–9, 83
'At a Potato Digging', 10, 30, 36
'At the Water's Edge', 56
'The Barn', 10, 15, 21, 72
'Blackberry Picking', 10, 15
'Bogland', 34–5, 89
'Bog Oak', 35–6, 45
'Broagh', 23, 25–7, 49
'Casualty', 57–8
'Changes', 74
'Churning Day', 10–11, 29
'Clearances', 75–7, 79
'A Constable Calls', 3
'Cow in Calf', 10
'The Crossing', 84
'Crossings', 84
'Dawn Shoot', 10, 15
Death of a Naturalist, 8–10, 13, 15–18, 20, 28, 30, 34, 70, 72, 77, 83
'Death of a Naturalist', 9–10, 15
'Digging', 8–9, 10, 12–15, 19, 28, 29, 33
'The Diviner', 70
'Docker', 32
Door into the Dark, 10, 18, 20, 22–3, 29–32, 34
'Elegy', 80
'Exposure', 4, 50–4, 69–70
'Field of Vision', 82–3
Field Work, 4, 54–61, 63, 69–73, 89
'The Folk Singers', 1
'Follower', 13–15, 70, 77
'The Forge' 10, 20–3, 70

'For the Commander of the *Eliza*', 30–1
'From the Land of the Unspoken', 67
'From the Republic of Conscience', 67, 90
'Funeral Rites', 39–43, 46, 49, 67
'Gifts of Rain', 23, 25
'Glanmore Sonnets', 69–73, 75, 79
The Government of the Tongue, 1–2, 5–7, 10, 68, 85–6, 87
The Haw Lantern, 75–7, 83
'A Hazel Stick for Catherine Ann', 73–5, 83
'Honeymoon Flight', 17
'In Illo Tempore', 63
'In Small Townlands', 10, 30
'The King of the Ditchbacks', 80–2
'Kinship, 33–4, 44–5
'A Kite for Michael and Christopher', 73–5
'Lightenings', 85
'Lovers on Aran', 17
'Man and Boy', 77–8
'Nerthus', 37–8
New Selected Poems, 8
'A New Song', 23, 25–7
North, 4, 28, 33, 39–47, 48, 50–4, 59, 69, 89
'A Northern Hoard', 50
'Ocean's Love to Ireland', 45–6
'The Old Icons', 67
An Open Letter, 88
'Orange Drums, Tyrone, 1966', 46
'The Otter', 73
'Personal Helicon', 20, 34
'A Postcard from North Antrim', 58, 64
Preoccupations, 8, 12, 13–14, 23, 26, 31–3
'Punishment', 42–3, 45, 49, 59
The Redress of Poetry, 88
'Remembering Malibu', 89
'Requiem for the Croppies', 30–2, 38
'Rite of Spring', 10,18
Seeing Things, 6, 67, 75, 77–8, 82–6
Selected Poems, 8
'Sybil', 56
'The Singer's House', 6
'The Skunk', 73, 89
Station Island, 54, 58–68, 73–5, 80, 89

'Station Island', 58–67
'The Strand at Lough Beg', 58–60
'Synge on Aran', 18–19
'Terminus', 83–4
'Thatcher', 10, 22–3, 70
'The Tollund Man', 37–9
'Toome', 23, 25
'The Toome Road', 54–6
'Triptych', 55–7, 65
'Trout', 29–30
'The Unacknowledged Legislator's Dream', 51–2
'The Underground', 73
'Undine', 18
'Westering', 89
'Whatever You Say, Say Nothing', 28, 44, 46
'Whinlands', 10
Wintering Out, 4, 20–3, 27, 28–9, 35, 37–9, 46, 50, 54, 89
Herbert, Zbigniew, 2, 5, 90
Hobsbaum, Philip, 8
Holub, Miroslav, 90
Homer
    The Iliad, 20–1
Hopkins, Gerard Manley, 9–10, 87
Hughes, Francis, 65–6
Hughes, Ted, 9–10, 87

Irish Republican Army (IRA), 55–8, 65, 88, 93

Joyce, James, 66–7
    Finnegans Wake, 66

Kavanagh, Patrick, 2–3, 10–11, 19–24, 80, 86, 87
    'Epic', 19–20
    The Great Hunger, 19
Keenan, Terry, 62
Kelly, Oisin, 70
King, Stephen, 88

Lloyd, David, 49–50, 53, 66
Longley, Edna
    Poetry in the Wars, 48
Longley, Michael, 28
Lowell, Robert, 89

Mandelstam, Osip, 50, 52
Marx, Karl, 36
McCartney, Colum, 58–60, 64
McGuinness, Frank, 67

Milosz, Czeslaw, 90
Moore, Marianne, 85–6
Morrison, Blake, 45, 88
  And When Did You Last See Your Father?, 79
Motion, Andrew, 88
Muldoon, Paul, 67

Nerthus, 37–8, 41, 44
Njal's Saga, 39–42, 49

O'Brien, Flann
  At Swim-Two-Birds, 80
O'Connor, Joseph, 89
O'Donoghue, Bernard, 39
O'Neill, Louis, 57–60

Parker, Michael, 16, 36, 37, 58, 89
Plath, Sylvia, 89

Ralegh, Walter, 45–6, 87
  'The Ocean's Love to Cynthia', 45
Rice, Anne, 88
Robinson, Mary, 91
Roethke, Theodore, 89

Saint John of the Cross (Juan de la Cruz), 63
Shakespeare, William, 87
  The Merchant of Venice, 72
Shelley, Percy, 51
Sidney, Philip, 79–80, 84
  Defence of Poetry, 22, 79
Simmons, James, 48, 53

Southey, Robert, 81
Spenser, Edmund, 35–6, 45, 87
  The Faerie Queene, 35
  A View of the Present State of Ireland, 35–6, 45
Strathern, William, 64–5
Sweeney, Simon, 61–2
Synge, John Millington, 18

Tacitus, Publius Cornelius
  Agricola, 44
  Germanica, 44
Toibín, Colm, 89
Toríacht Diarmuida agus Grainne, 72

Virgil, 59
  Aeneid, 77–8, 84

Waterman, Andrew, 11
Welch, Robert, 22
Wordsworth, Dorothy, 71
Wordsworth, William, 71
  'Tintern Abbey', 74
Wyatt, Thomas, 87
  'They fle from me . . .', 73

Yeats, William Butler, 79, 87, 90
  'Easter 1916', 4
  'In Memory of Major Robert Gregory', 4–5
  'Meditations in Time of Civil War', 4
  'The Rose Tree', 4
  'September 1913', 4

Recent and
Forthcoming Titles
in the
New Series of

WRITERS AND
THEIR WORK

WRITERS AND THEIR WORK

RECENT & FORTHCOMING TITLES

Title	Author
W.H. Auden	*Stan Smith*
Aphra Behn	*Sue Wiseman*
Lord Byron	*J. Drummond Bone*
Angela Carter	*Lorna Sage*
Geoffrey Chaucer	*Steve Ellis*
Children's Literature	*Kimberley Reynolds*
John Clare	*John Lucas*
Joseph Conrad	*Cedric Watts*
John Donne	*Stevie Davies*
Henry Fielding	*Jenny Uglow*
Elizabeth Gaskell	*Kate Flint*
William Golding	*Kevin McCarron*
Graham Greene	*Peter Mudford*
Hamlet	*Ann Thompson & Neil Taylor*
Thomas Hardy	*Peter Widdowson*
David Hare	*Jeremy Ridgman*
Tony Harrison	*Joe Kelleher*
William Hazlitt	*J.B. Priestley; R.L. Brett (introduction by Michael Foot)*
Seamus Heaney	*Andrew Murphy*
George Herbert	*T.S. Eliot (introduction by Peter Porter)*
Henry James - The Later Writing	*Barbara Hardy*
James Joyce	*Steven Connor*
King Lear	*Terence Hawkes*
Doris Lessing	*Elizabeth Maslen*
David Lodge	*Bernard Bergonzi*
Christopher Marlowe	*Thomas Healy*
Andrew Marvell	*Annabel Patterson*
Ian McEwan	*Kiernan Ryan*
A Midsummer Night's Dream	*Helen Hackett*
Walter Pater	*Laurel Brake*
Jean Rhys	*Helen Carr*
Dorothy Richardson	*Carol Watts*
The Sensation Novel	*Lyn Pykett*
Edmund Spenser	*Colin Burrow*
J.R.R. Tolkien	*Charles Moseley*
Leo Tolstoy	*John Bayley*
Virginia Woolf	*Laura Marcus*
Charlotte Yonge	*Alethea Hayter*

TITLES IN PREPARATION

Title	Author
Peter Ackroyd	*Susana Onega*
Antony and Cleopatra	*Ken Parker*
Jane Austen	*Robert Clark*
Samuel Beckett	*Keir Elam*
William Blake	*John Beer*
Elizabeth Bowen	*Maud Ellmann*
Emily Brontë	*Stevie Davies*
A.S. Byatt	*Richard Todd*
Caryl Churchill	*Elaine Aston*
S.T. Coleridge	*Stephen Bygrave*
Crime Fiction	*Martin Priestman*
Charles Dickens	*Rod Mengham*
Carol Ann Duffy	*Deryn Rees Jones*
Daniel Defoe	*Jim Rigney*
George Eliot	*Josephine McDonagh*
E.M. Forster	*Nicholas Royle*
Brian Friel	*Geraldine Higgins*
Henry IV	*Peter Bogdanov*
Henrik Ibsen	*Sally Ledger*
Rudyard Kipling	*Jan Montefiore*
Franz Kafka	*Michael Wood*
John Keats	*Kelvin Everest*
Philip Larkin	*Laurence Lerner*
D.H. Lawrence	*Linda Ruth Williams*
Measure for Measure	*Kate Chedgzoy*
William Morris	*Anne Janowitz*
Brian Patten	*Linda Cookson*
Alexander Pope	*Pat Rogers*
Sylvia Plath	*Elizabeth Bronfen*
Richard II	*Margaret Healy*
Lord Rochester	*Peter Porter*
Romeo and Juliet	*Sasha Roberts*
Christina Rossetti	*Kathryn Burlinson*
Salman Rushdie	*Damian Grant*
Sir Walter Scott	*John Sutherland*
Stevie Smith	*Alison Light*
Wole Soyinka	*Mpalive Msiska*
Laurence Sterne	*Manfred Pfister*
Jonathan Swift	*Claude Rawson*
The Tempest	*Gordon McMullan*
Mary Wollstonecraft	*Jane Moore*
Evelyn Waugh	*Malcolm Bradbury*
John Webster	*Thomas Sorge*
Angus Wilson	*Peter Conradi*
William Wordsworth	*Nicholas Roe*
Working Class Fiction	*Ian Haywood*
W.B. Yeats	*Ed Larrissy*

JOHN CLARE

John Lucas

Setting out to recover Clare – whose work was demeaned and damaged by the forces of the literary establishment – as a great poet, John Lucas offers the reader the chance to see the life and work of John Clare, the 'peasant poet' from a new angle. His unique and detailed study portrays a knowing, articulate and radical poet and thinker writing as much out of a tradition of song as of poetry. This is a comprehensive and detailed account of the man and the artist which conveys a strong sense of the writer's social and historical context.

"Clare's unique greatness is asserted and proved in John Lucas's brilliant, sometimes moving, discourse." **Times Educational Supplement.**

John Lucas has written many books on nineteenth- and twentieth-century literature, and is himself a talented poet. He is Professor of English at Loughborough University.

0 7463 0729 2 paperback 96pp

GEORGE HERBERT

T.S. Eliot

With a new introductory essay by **Peter Porter**

Another valuable reissue from the original series, this important study – one of T. S. Eliot's last critical works – examines the writings of George Herbert, considered by Eliot to be one of the loveliest and most profound of English poets. The new essay by well-known poet and critic Peter Porter reassesses Eliot's study, as well as providing a new perspective on Herbert's work. Together, these critical analyses make an invaluable contribution to the available literature on this major English poet.

0 7463 0746 2 paperback 80pp £5.99

CHILDREN'S LITERATURE

Kimberley Reynolds

Children's literature has changed dramatically in the last hundred years and this book identifies and analyses the dominant genres which have evolved during this period. Drawing on a wide range of critical and cultural theories, Kimberley Reynolds looks at children's private reading, examines the relationship between the child reader and the adult writer, and draws some interesting conclusions about children's literature as a forum for shaping the next generation and as a safe place for developing writers' private fantasies.

"The book manages to cover a surprising amount of ground . . . without ever seeming perfunctory. It is a very useful book in an area where a short pithy introduction like this is badly needed." **Times Educational Supplement**

Kimberley Reynolds lectures in English and Women's Studies at Roehampton Institute, where she also runs the Children's Literature Research Unit.

0 7463 0728 4 paperback 112pp

HENRY FIELDING
Jenny Uglow

In this fresh introduction to his work, Uglow looks at Fielding in his own historical context and in the light of recent critical debates. She identifies and clarifies many of Fielding's central ideas, such as those of judgement, benevolence and mercy which became themes in his novels. Looking not only at the novels, but also at Fielding's drama, essays, journalism and political writings, Uglow traces the author's development, clarifies his ideas on his craft, and provides a fascinating insight into eighteenth-century politics and society.

Jenny Uglow is a critic and publisher.

0 7463 0751 9 paperback 96pp

HENRY JAMES
The Later Writing
Barbara Hardy

Barbara Hardy focuses on Henry James's later works, dating from 1900 to 1916. Offering new readings of the major novels and a re-evaluation of the criticism to date, she considers language and theme in a number of Jamesian works, including *The Ambassadors, The Wings of the Dove* and *The Golden Bowl,* and engages with his autobiographical and travel writing and literary criticism. Hardy's analysis traces two dominant themes – the social construction of character and the nature of creative imagination – and reveals James to be a disturbing analyst of inner life.

Barbara Hardy is Professor Emeritus at Birkbeck College, University of London.

0 7463 0748 9 paperback 96pp

DAVID LODGE
Bernard Bergonzi

Internationally celebrated as both a novelist and a literary critic, David Lodge is one of Britain's most successful and influential living writers. He has been instrumental in introducing and explaining modern literary theory to British readers while maintaining, in regard to his own work, "faith in the future of realistic fiction". Bergonzi's up-to-date and comprehensive study covers both Lodge's critical writing as well as his novels of the past 35 years (from *The Picturegoers* to *Therapy*) and explores how he expresses and convincingly combines metafiction, realism, theology and dazzling comedy.

Bernard Bergonzi is Emeritus Professor of English at the University of Warwick.

0 7463 0755 1 paperback 80pp

DAVID HARE
Jeremy Ridgman

David Hare is one of the most prolific, challenging, and culturally acclaimed playwrights in Britain today. Jeremy Ridgman's study focuses on the dramatic method that drives the complex moral and political narratives of Hare's work. He considers its relationship to its staging and performance, looking in particular at the dramatist's collaborations with director, designer, and performer. Hare's writing for the theatre since 1970 is set alongside his work for television and film and his achievements as director and translator, to provide a detailed insight into key areas of his dramatic technique particularly dialogue, narrative, and epic form.

Jeremy Ridgman is Senior Lecturer in the Department of Drama and Theatre Studies at Roehampton Institute, London

0 7463 0774 8 paperback 96pp

TONY HARRISON
Joe Kelleher

Tony Harrison has been acclaimed worldwide, not only for his slim volumes of poetry but also for his lyric sequences and long poems, for his adaptations and original plays for the theatre, his opera libretti, and his verse films for television. Kelleher argues that Harrison's unique achievement is to ransack a whole range of traditions in order to carve out in verse, a very innovative and contemporary mode of public utterance.

Joe Kelleher is a playwright and Lecturer in Drama at Roehampton Institute.

0 7463 0789 6 paperback 96pp

CHARLOTTE YONGE
Alethea Hayter

Charlotte Yonge was a best-selling Victorian author and widely admired by her greatest literary contemporaries in the mid-nineteenth century but for the next hundred years, ignored or vilified by critics. Her work has only recently begun to receive the attention it deserves from biographers, historians and feminists. Alethea Hayter's appraisal of Yonge as a writer surveys the full range of her work – her non-fictional studies in history and wild-life, as well as her family chronicles, historical novels and children's books. Yonge emerges as a perceptive writer who well deserves the renewed interest in her and her work.

Alethea Hayter is a literary critic and historian, who has pubished a number of books on nineteenth-century literature.

0 7463 0781 0 paperback 96pp

ELIZABETH GASKELL

Kate Flint

Recent critical appraisal has focused on Gaskell both as a novelist of industrial England and on her awareness of the position of women and the problems of the woman writer. Kate Flint reveals how for Gaskell the condition of women was inseparable from broader issues of social change. She shows how recent modes of feminist criticism and theories of narrative illuminate the radicalism and experimentalism which we find in Gaskell's fiction.

Kate Flint is University Lecturer in Victorian and Modern English Literature, and Fellow of Linacre College, Oxford.

0 7463 0718 7paperback 96pp

LEO TOLSTOY

John Bayley

Leo Tolstoy's writing remains as lively, as fascinating, and as absorbing as ever and continues to have a profound influence on imaginative writing. This original and elegant study serves as an introduction to Tolstoy, concentrating on his two greatest novels – *War and Peace* and *Anna Karenina* – and the ancillary texts and tales that relate to them. By examining how Tolstoy created a uniquely spacious and complex fictional world, John Bayley provides a fascinating analysis of the novels, explaining why they continue to delight and inform readers today.

John Bayley is Warton Professor of English Emeritus at St Catherine's College, University of Oxford.

0 7463 0744 6 paperback 96pp

EDMUND SPENSER

Colin Burrow

Considered by many to be the greatest Elizabethan poet, Edmund Spenser's writing has inspired both admiration and bewilderment. The grace of Spenser's language and his skilful and enchanting evocation of the fairy world have, for many, been offset by the sheer bulk and complexity of his work. Colin Burrow's considered and highly readable account provides a reading of Spenser which clarifies the genres and conventions used by the writer. Burrow explores the poet's taste for archaism and allegory, his dual attraction to images of vital rebirth and mortal frailty, and his often conflictual relationship with his Queen and with the Irish landscape in which he spent his mature years.

Colin Burrow is Fellow, Tutor and College Lecturer in English at Gonville & Caius College, University of Cambridge.

0 7463 0750 0 paperback 128pp